GREAT INVENTIONS

# Clocks

Domine Salvam fac Reginam nostram Victoriam

GREAT INVENTIONS

# Clocks

JAMES LINCOLN COLLIER

BENCHMARK BOOKS
MARSHALL CAVENDISH
NEW YORK

*The author would like to thank Michael Lash, acting director of the National Time Museum, for his careful reading of the text and for his thoughtful and useful comments. The work has been much improved by his help. The author, however, assumes all responsibility for whatever errors may appear.*

Benchmark Books
Marshall Cavendish
99 White Plains Road
Tarrytown, NY 10591-9001
www.marshallcavendish.com

Illustrations by Janet Hamlin


Library of Congress Cataloging-in-Publication Data

Collier, James Lincoln, 1928-
The clock / James Lincoln Collier.
v. cm.— (Great inventions)
Includes bibliographical references and index.
Contents: Since the beginning of time—Timekeeping marches on—The great escapement—Springs and pendulums—Setting the year straight—Navigation time— Time for everybody—Atomic time for an atomic world.

ISBN 0-7614-1538-6

1. Clocks and watches—History—Juvenile literature. [1. Clocks and watches. 2. Time measurements.] I. Title. II. Series: Great inventions (Benchmark Books (Firm))

TS542.5.C65 2003
681.1'13—dc21
2002156288

Photo research by James Lincoln Collier

Series Design by Sonia Chaghatzbanian

Cover photo: Royalty Free/Corbis

The photographs in this book are used by permission and through the courtesy of: *Corbis*: 94; Royalty Free, 2; Adam Woolfitt, 14, 124-125; Lindsay Hebberd, 18; Jonathan Blair, 28; Bettmann, 62, 103, 104; Elio Ciol, 64; Archivo Iconografico, S.A., 67; The Corcoran Gallery of Art, 68; Michael Freeman, 78; Historical Picture Archive, 81; Gianni Dagli Orti, 90, 92. *The John Hardy Collection*: 8. *New York Public Library*: 12, 21, 29, 30, 33, 34, 56, 72, 76, 82, 99. *Science Museum, London*: 24, 39, 44, 50, 54, 59, 84, 108, 111. *James Lincoln Collier*: 89.

Printed in China

1 3 5 6 4 2

# Contents

GREAT INVENTIONS

# Clocks

The importance we place on measuring time is suggested by the fact that, unlike many of our other tools, watches are often designed to be attractive, carefully styled, and very expensive. Almost from the beginning, watches and clocks were used to indicate status, as are these watches designed by John Hardy.

ONE

# Since the Beginning of Time

Time is one of the great mysteries. We cannot touch it, see it, or hear it; but we know that it is somehow "passing," going by us just as surely as the wind passes us on a breezy day. What is it? Since the beginning of recorded history, people have struggled to understand this crucial dimension of life. Some cultures, such as our Western culture, take the approach that time is like a stream, moving endlessly in one direction. Other cultures, as for example the Hindus of India, see time as a wheel, which revolves for thousands of years, but always comes back to the same starting point. Other cultures have yet other ideas about time.

However we may look at it, our awareness that we live in the dimension of time, as we do in a world with height and width, is an essential part of ourselves. We are, mostly, thoroughly aware that we have a past "behind" us and a future "ahead" of us. Indeed, we might be more certain of our pasts and futures than we are of the "present," a point in the stream of time that neither scientists nor philosophers have ever satisfactorily defined. What we do in the future is very much colored by our experiences. For example, if the stock we bought last year has risen in value, we are likely to buy more; if it has lost value, we will not. Indeed, even the way we think about ourselves is colored by our past: if the stock we bought has risen, we congratulate ourselves for our wisdom; if it has fallen, we curse ourselves for our stupidity.

Time matters to us deeply. Thus, it is hardly surprising that human beings have, for thousands of years, tried to figure out how to count it, to discover how much of it has passed, how much of it is left, and to learn when it began and when it will end, if ever.

When did humans first start thinking about time? We cannot be sure. The first humans emerged on the plains of Africa several million years ago. They walked upright and gradually learned to use rough tools, if only sticks and stones to throw at game and their enemies. Over time newer human forms developed, generally smarter and better at making tools. Some scientists believe that these successive human types also developed in Africa and spread around the world from there. About 100,000 years ago, modern humans appeared. Far and away the smartest creatures the world had ever seen, they blossomed and spread out of Africa, moving west and north into what is now Europe, and eastward into the Middle East, Russia, Asia, and eventually the Americas.

These creatures rapidly improved their tool-making skills. Particularly adept was a group that had moved into Europe, especially the areas around what is now France and Spain. Between roughly 40,000 and 10,000 years ago, these people established a rich hunting and gathering culture, based on their ability to kill big game, such as various types of deer, oxen, mammoths, and others. They learned to make barbed bone harpoon heads for spearing fish, needles for sewing together animal skins to make shelters and clothing, and a wide array of cutting and chopping tools.

These people were nomadic, we believe, moving through a known territory to follow herds of animals that migrated through the seasons, to visit berrying grounds when the fruit was ripe, or to fish streams when the salmon were running.

Their environment was rich enough to allow them time to create art and practice religion. From footprints hardened in the mud of cave floors, we know that they danced; from bone flutes, we know they had music; from thousands of wall paintings, we know that they had, if not organized religion, at least ceremonies, rites, rituals, and mythical lore and legend.

Could they tell time? Undoubtedly, they had a sense of the past and the future—their brains were much like ours. But could they measure time? It clearly would have been a great advantage to them to know when the salmon were likely to run or how long it would be until the first snow fell. But the fact that a certain skill or type of knowledge would be useful to humans does not mean that they acquired it: humans sought ways to fly thousands of years before they were actually able to do so.

Nonetheless, some paleoanthropologists believe that these ancient people did have ways of telling time. They must certainly have noticed the cycles of the moon and possibly figured out that each one lasted about twenty-nine days. In Europe where there are obvious changes in the seasons, they must have grasped the cycle we call the year, which went round and round in predictable fashion. They also might have figured out the solstices, the shortest and longest days of the year, and possibly the equinoxes, the day each spring and fall when day and night are equal. We are, of course, only guessing, but there is some archeological evidence that these people had rough calendars. A piece of bone about 30,000 years old, found in France, bears scratch marks, which some investigators believe were meant to indicate the cycles of the moon. A few similar stone calendars have been found as well. However, other archeologists insist that such marks on stone or bone may have been decorations or mere paleological doodles. There is no definite proof either way.

But if humans were not yet able to measure time, they were about to be. There have been two monumental changes in human life since the days of the hunting-and-gathering tribes that covered the earth for so long and still exist today in a few small pockets. One of these changes was the Industrial Revolution, which we shall look at later. Before that was the Neolithic Revolution, which started about 10,000 years ago. This was a shift from the hunting-gathering lifestyle to farming. (The term *Neolithic Age* means "new stone age.") So far as paleoanthropologists have been able to piece evidence together, the Neolithic Revolution started when hunters began systematically controlling the herds of animals they hunted, directing their travels so as to

These Neolithic dancers painted on a rock may have had religious or magical significance. Early human cultures were rich in art and ceremony. It is quite likely they had worked out rough calendar systems as well.

have some always on hand for food. The next step was to cultivate the grasses the animals and humans fed on, planting it in convenient places. In time they began cultivating plants and animals for better growth and to improve them by selective breeding. Farming had arrived.

Farming, however, meant staying put instead of wandering through fields and forests, simply because a field left untended would be plundered by birds and beasts and be taken over by weeds. Staying put brought its own great advantages. For one thing, nomadic bands could carry with them only modest tool kits, but a settled people could develop an extensive array of tools for special purposes which could be set aside in a corner of the shelter to be brought out when needed. More elaborate shelters could be built, along with special buildings designed for storage. This meant that in a good year excess grain and other foodstuffs could be put aside to carry the band through a time of scarcity. The need for storage in turn hastened the need for one of the great inventions of Neolithic times, pottery. Heavy pots, which were easily broken, were of little use to nomads. For farming people they were essential for holding grain and especially liquids such as water, oil, honey, beer, and berry juices. They could be used for cooking, too, which made it possible for these Neolithic people to stew root vegetables and other tough foods to make them edible, thus broadening their diet.

The Neolithic Age was indeed revolutionary. Human beings began to live in small settlements, some of which in time grew into towns or even what might be described as cities. The human population, with the more abundant food supply produced by farming, grew rapidly. A surplus of food allowed at least some people in these settlements or little towns to work at nonessential trades such as bracelet and brooch makers, wood carvers, priests, and students of the movement of the celestial bodies—the Sun, Moon, planets, and stars. A culture far surpassing that of the cave painters of 15,000 years before emerged.

As a result of the new pockets of prosperity, skirmishes and squabbles grew. Fighting became war. Tribes whose crops had failed, or who were simply jealous of the wealth of a more successful group, would make hit-and-run raids, hoping to seize animals, weapons, tools, and even prisoners. People in settlements learned to build fortifications—walls, ditches, and palisades. Life began to assume a form somewhat similar to ours.

To ensure their group's success, farmers needed to know, if not the time of day, at least the time of the year. To some extent they could be guided by natural signs. But there were cases when natural signs were not a dependable guide. Farmers in more northern or southern areas had to know the earliest moment in the spring when there was little chance of a killing frost, so they could plant as soon as possible to ensure a long growing season. They needed to know, for example, when to move animals into

In many places in Europe, particularly in the British Isles, huge stone structures called megaliths were built by Neolithic peoples. This megalith at Callanish on the island of Lewis off the western coast of Scotland seems to indicate the equinoxes and the solstices.

winter quarters and when breeding time was about to arrive. Natural signs were not always reliable. Farmers need calendars.

During Neolithic times humans began to work out ways of knowing where they were in the progression of the year. From about 5000 B.C. to 1500 B.C., and even later, Neolithic people in what is now the British Isles, but also elsewhere in Europe, built several hundred arrangements of stone, mostly huge constructions called megaliths. They were usually, but not always, in the form of large circles of upright stone slabs, with perhaps other features, such as lintels running across the tops of the upright slabs. The most famous of these megalithic structures is Stonehenge in England, in part made of stones, some weighing several tons each, which somehow had to be transported 137 miles (220 km) from the Precelly Mountains in South

Wales. Stonehenge was built and rebuilt several times from 3100 B.C. to 1600 B.C. Some scientists claim that many of the stones in it line up to indicate important celestial events—the solstices, the equinoxes, and other cosmic alignments. Similar claims have been made for the other megalithic structures as well.

Some archeologists object to such interpretations and insist that the placement of the stones indicating a solstice or equinox was accidental. Yet there are some structures that seem clearly intended to permanently mark one of the year's annual signal points. At New Grange, north of Dublin, Ireland, there is a Neolithic tomb from about 3300 B.C. with an opening which allows a beam of light to fall on a certain carving at the back of the tomb at sunrise on the day of the winter solstice. Similar structures have been found in South America's Andes Mountains and elsewhere. It is generally agreed, then, that at least in Neolithic times humans had some grasp of the movement of celestial bodies and were using these as calendars.

By Neolithic times, if not before, human beings had come to realize that the measurement of time has a great deal to do with the movement of celestial bodies. They first comprehended that the cycles of the planets, stars, Sun, Moon, and Earth were regular and unchanging. Indeed, they were among the few immutable things in the unpredictable lives early humans lived, with its often unhappy surprises of hailstorms, sudden attacks, drought, and illness. And ever since, we have continued to tell time in good measure from the movement of the heavens.

Astronomy—the study of celestial bodies—is a vast and often complex subject, dealing as it does with such concepts as the speed of light and the origins of the universe. It has always fascinated humans. Some of the greatest astrophysicists began as stargazers in their childhood—peering up at the planets with small telescopes. In a short book such as this, we will only touch on some basic matters. First of all, as many readers already know, Earth rotates on its own axis each day in a period of time we divide into twenty-four hours. However, Earth does not stand up straight, if we may put it that way. The axis on which it spins, a line from the North to the South Poles, is not perpendicular to a line drawn from the Sun to Earth, but tilts a little. If you take a ball and walk it around an exposed light bulb, you can demonstrate this principle. As Earth passes around the Sun, first one pole and then the next is tilted toward the Sun, the other away from it. When the North Pole is leaning in, the sun covers more of the Northern Hemisphere than the Southern Hemisphere, and vice versa. This has two effects. For one, it causes the seasons, in part because the hemisphere leaning in spends more time in the Sun each day, and in part because the Sun's rays strike it more directly. A second effect is that the hemisphere that is tilted inward experiences longer days and shorter nights.

Obviously, as Earth continues to tilt back and forth in its annual progress around the Sun, twice each year it reaches a point where neither hemisphere is favored. We call these days the spring and fall equinoxes, when night and day are equal in length. They are called the vernal, meaning spring, and autumnal equinoxes, and occur in March and September on slightly different days due to leap years, which add an extra day to the year every four years.

Equally as essential to an understanding of time are the two days in the year when the tilt reaches its farthest point in either direction. These days are known as the summer and winter solstices and come in June (midsummer's night) and December. Most calendars give the dates for the equinoxes and solstices each year. These are important days that we will hear a good deal about in the course of this book.

Another key celestial event is the revolution of the Moon around Earth, or as it appeared to early humans, the nightly trip of the Moon across the sky. They would certainly have noticed the monthly waxing and waning of the moon as it bloomed into the full moon and then began to grow slim and eventually disappear. It is probable that Neolithic humans understood something of the motions of the stars and planets as well. They may have noticed—in the Northern Hemisphere at least—that the North Star appears to be fixed and unmoving, and therefore a guide to travel by at night.

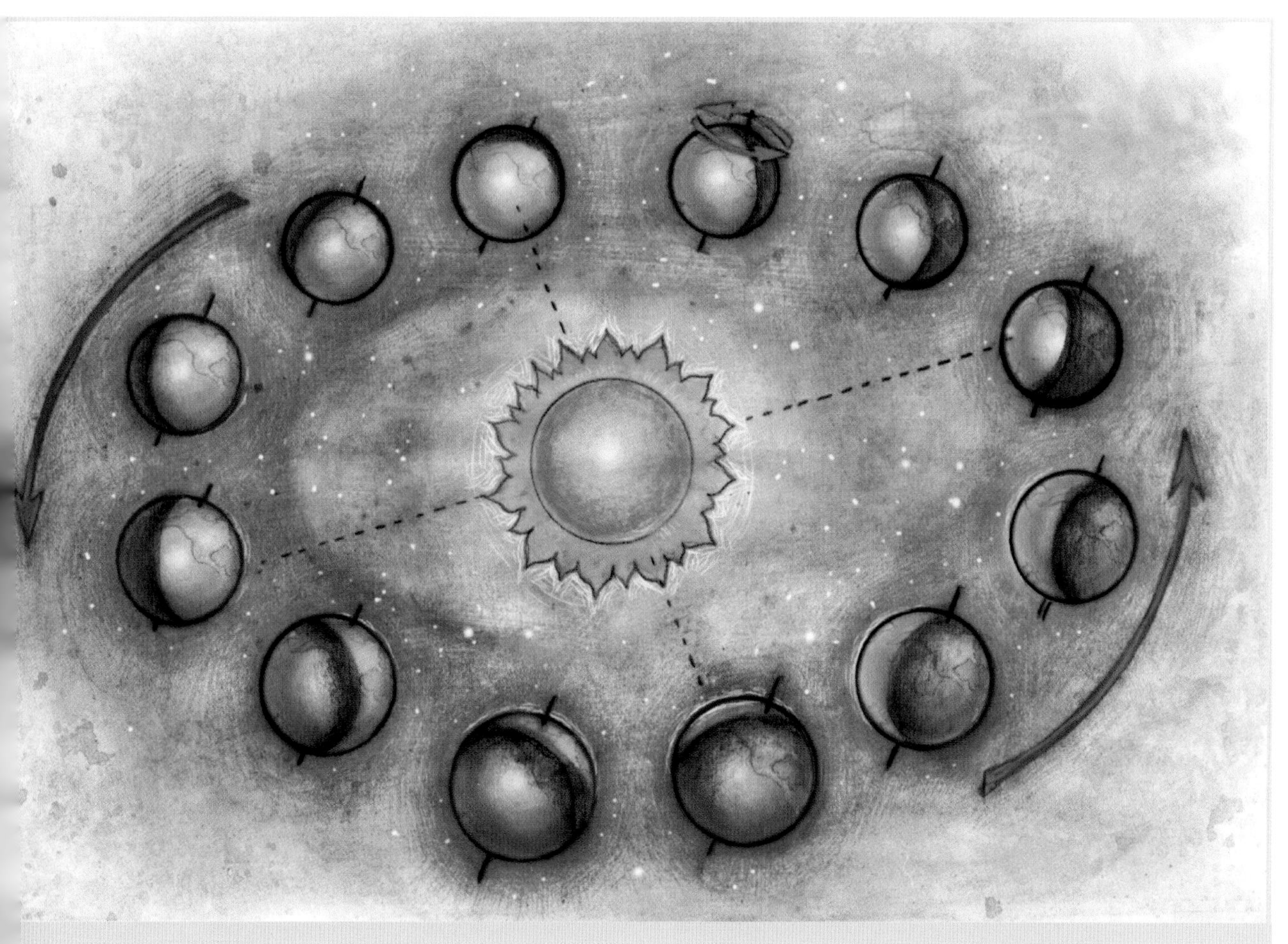

Seasons are caused by the changing tilt of Earth's axis in relation to the Sun. When the Earth is in the position on the left, the North Pole is angled toward the Sun. More of the planet's Northern Hemisphere receives sunlight during the days, which are longer, while the nights are shorter. Summer occurs because more of the Sun's rays penetrate the atmosphere. When Earth is in the position pictured on the right, the South Pole is angled toward the Sun and winter occurs in the Northern Hemisphere, while it is summer in the southern part of the globe. Finally, when Earth is in the positions at the top and bottom of the illustration, we experience the equinoxes. Though Earth is still tilted to one side, the North and South Poles are the same distance from the Sun, so both hemispheres get the same amount of sunlight, with night and day each twelve hours long.

AN EARLY OBSERVATORY IN NEW DELHI, INDIA, HAD CALIBRATIONS ON THE WALLS AND FLOORS BY WHICH THE HORIZONTAL AND VERTICAL ANGLES OF THE MOON AND STARS COULD BE READ. THE SLANTING STRUCTURE IN THE BACKGROUND IS A LARGE SUNDIAL. INTEREST IN ASTRONOMY HAS BEEN INTENSE THROUGHOUT HUMAN HISTORY. HUMANS HAVE LONG USED CELESTIAL MOTION TO NAVIGATE AND TO MEASURE TIME.

They may also have noticed that the point on the eastern horizon where certain stars appeared each night drifted farther along the horizon day by day. But undoubtedly far more important to them was the passing of the year, with its seasons, solstices, and equinoxes, the comings and goings of night and day, and the waxing and waning of the Moon.

And here is where the problems arose for calendar makers that took thousands of years to solve: these movements are incommensurate—that is, they do not relate to each other in a simple mathematical way. Earth makes its way around the Sun in about 11 minutes short of 365 days. The Moon makes its passage from full to new and to full again in 29.531 days on average, but there is some variation from month to month. You cannot, thus, divide the year into equal months, nor into equal days. This problem would give timekeepers fits for millennia. The cosmos simply was not as tidy as humans would have liked. We shall learn of the struggles people have gone through to neaten it up.

TWO

# Timekeeping Marches On

Much of the progress in timekeeping took place in Europe—indeed in western Europe. But the start was made in the Middle East, where great civilizations arose 2,000 years before the Neolithic people of the British Isles were building Stonehenge.

Most people understand the world primarily visually, through eyesight. Of course we take in information with our other senses—touch, hearing, smell, even taste. But our main dependence is on sight. For example, our ability to turn audible talk into visual writing brought an extraordinarily sweeping change to human life, for it allowed us to carry words from place to place, to preserve them for long periods of time, and to reconsider and reorganize them in a way that would be difficult, if not impossible, in simple conversation.

Thus, right from the beginning, people concerned with measuring time tried to make it visible. Making the months and years visible was relatively easy. A day, which was marked by clearly visible events, such as the sunrise and sunset, had clear beginnings. A scratch mark of some kind on a bone, stone, piece of wood, or even the ground could stand for a day, and days could thus be scored off one after another and counted to make up a larger unit of time—a week, month, year, or decade.

Measuring the time passing through a day was a more difficult matter, for it did not break down into small units, beyond the change from day to

The first civilizations, founded in Mesopotamia, developed writing, wheeled vehicles, and complex notions of astrological systems among other things. By the eighth century B.C., Assyria had ox-drawn chariots like this one carved into the walls of the city.

night and back again. At the outset, those measuring time made an obvious and wholly natural mistake. Time appeared to flow like a liquid. In measuring time, then, they went in search of something that flowed, with which to make time visible. It would be several thousand years before the mistake was corrected.

We only begin to know with confidence about the attempts to measure time with the invention of writing by the Sumerians, who inhabited the area around the Tigris and Euphrates Rivers in what is now Iraq, an area previously called Mesopotamia, long known as the cradle of civilization. More recent studies of the past several decades suggest that this burgeoning civilization extended into an even larger area. Excavations at Catal Hüyük in Turkey and at Jericho, in what is now Israel, have uncovered cities dating back to 6000 B.C. or earlier. These very early centers had all the trappings of civilization—pottery, metal, religion, myths, temples, taxes, and, of course, war. We assume that they had calendars as well, but no examples have been found.

But we have evidence of many Sumerian advances. The Sumerians devised the first wheeled vehicles in about 3500 B.C., and in 3200 B.C. they began to develop cuneiform, the first known system of writing. By 2500 B.C. they had a numbering system akin to ours, except that it was built on the base sixty, rather than our base ten.

Sumer was a complex society with at least four major walled cities, centered on temples. Around the cities were pastures, fields, and villages watered by irrigation systems. The Sumerians needed a government and laws, which meant they needed judges, soldiers, government officials, and priests. As state religion found a role in society, they needed priests. To pay the taxes that had to be raised to fund government services, there had to be a surplus of grain, meat, cloth, and everything else produced each year. A civilization such as Sumer could not possibly function without good systems for measuring time. The rulers had to know when taxes should be collected, when debts had to be paid, and when government officials and soldiers needed to get their wages. They had to be able to divide the day so as to set working hours. In addition, they had to know what days were sacred and when people should be called together to worship. The needs of religious leaders to know these dates and times turned out to be critical to the creation of calendars and clocks.

Inevitably, the Sumerians were deeply concerned with the movements of the celestial bodies. Their concern was not solely for determining the months, the year, and the solstices: it is also probable that, like many people, even in the United States today, they believed that the stars controlled destiny, even though no evidence existed (or exists now) to support such a belief. Nevertheless, they believed that the heavens had to be charted to help rulers make predictions. Among other things, the Sumerians, with their belief that the number 60 was especially important, divided the circle into 360 degrees, a system we still use today. They also divided the day into twelve hours, a number related to both 60 and 360, with each hour being twice as long as our standard hour today. They further divided this hour into sixty minutes and the minute into sixty seconds, although it was doubtful that they could actually measure these small units.

The Sumerian civilization was eventually swallowed up by the Babylonians. They are thought to have divided the day into twenty-four hours, with twelve daylight hours and twelve nighttime hours. They kept the Sumerian system of dividing an hour into sixty minutes and the minute into sixty seconds. They also went on to develop the first documented instruments for measuring time, although the Sumerians, or other people, may have had similar instruments that did not survive.

One of these instruments is still with us today. It is the gnomon (pronounced NO-mon), a rod set up to cast a shadow on some sort of graduated ruler or measuring stick to indicate the hours or some other unit of time. The gnomon on a sundial is the one we are most familiar with, but there are other types. For example, if a short stick or rod is joined at a right angle to another one and set up facing away from the Sun, the vertical rod will cast a shadow on the horizontal one. The shadow shrinks as the Sun climbs towards noon and then begins to grow as the Sun heads towards the

THIS EGYPTIAN WATER CLOCK HAS A SMALL HOLE IN THE BOTTOM THROUGH WHICH THE LIQUID SLOWLY DRAINED OUT. LINES ON THE WALLS OF THE POT INDICATED THE HOURS, BUT THESE CLOCKS WERE OFTEN NOT VERY ACCURATE.

western horizon. Indeed, a tree, a building, a tower, anything straight and vertical can be used as a gnomon. The obelisks built in ancient Egypt and elsewhere were often used as gnomons. Figuring out how to mark the hours on a shadow timer takes a little knowledge of geometry, but the Babylonians knew enough general mathematics to do this.

But a sundial is of no use at night or on a cloudy day. Something else was needed to make the passage of time visible. The Babylonians discovered, or possibly inherited from another culture, the first important type of clock, which would still be used in the eighteenth century. This was the clepsydra, or water clock. Like time, water flows. The water clock worked on a very simple principle: water was allowed to drip into, or out of, a container. Lines or markings on the inside of the container would show the hours as the water rose or fell. Eventually some water clocks were fitted with floats that moved a needle up and down a scale to show the time.

The only problem was that when a container is full, the weight of the water drives the liquid out through a hole faster than when it is nearly empty, when the weight is much less. To counteract this, the container was made conical, or cone shaped, with the wide end pointing up. Thus, at first a greater amount of water had to flow out to drop the level the same distance as when the water was lower in the cone. Then less water dripped out to mark the similar length of time.

A second problem with water clocks was temperature. Water flows slower when it is cold. Moreover, in severe cold the clepsydra could actually freeze. Yet a more serious problem was the fact that days and nights grow longer and shorter during the year. To us that is not a problem: an hour is an hour whenever it comes. But to these ancient peoples—indeed well into the Middle Ages—day and night were not simply part of the same unit of time, but two different conditions or states. Night was not just the part of each day when it happened to be dark, but something of its own. We must remember, before the creation of cheap artificial light in the nineteenth century, people lived by the Sun. When it grew dark they often went to sleep, as their nighttime activities became limited.

Today, we often ignore the division between night and day, timing our lives by the clock—that is, we leave for work at seven, have supper at six, go to bed at ten, regardless of whether it is light or dark. These earlier people could not ignore the approach of night as we do: the traveler, fearful for his or her safety, would quicken the pace as the Sun began to droop towards the horizon, the worker would hurry to finish the job at hand so he could get home to eat his supper while there was still some light. Night and day had different qualities. Thus, there was a strong tendency to give each part of the day its own set of hours.

This was not a problem for Babylonians, who, as we have seen, divided the day into twelve equal hours. It was, however, a problem for the Egyptians, who were becoming the dominant power in the Middle East by about 3000 B.C. The Egyptians established the system of "unequal hours" which would last into the Middle Ages. Night and day each had their own set of twelve hours. But with night and day changing lengths as the year progressed, sundials and water clocks had to be changed too. In the end, the Egyptians never got their time-telling instruments right. Time remained for them a slippery commodity to measure.

These ancient peoples had similar problems with their calendars. As we have seen, the daily, monthly, and yearly cycles do not jibe. Twelve lunar months run about 354 days, or 11 days short of a year. The Babylonians solved the problem by adding a thirteenth month to some years. The Egyptians used twelve 30-day months, which came out to 360 days, to which they added an extra five days. However, that left a quarter of a day unaccounted for, and over time the Egyptian calendar began to slide slowly ahead of the actual year.

The Babylonians may also have been the first to settle on the seven-day week; they believed that the seventh, fourteenth, twenty-first, and twenty-eighth days of the month were unlucky. Some scholars have concluded that this idea led to the establishment of a week.

The Sumerian, Babylonian, and Egyptian civilizations of the Middle East did make some headway in understanding the Sun, the stars, and the planets. However, a true understanding of the motions of the universe began with the great philosophers of ancient Greece, such as Aristotle and Plato, after 500 B.C. Some Greeks came to understand many of the key facts about the celestial bodies, for example, that the moon got its light from the Sun and that Earth was curved, even spherical. They worked out celestial measurements, such as the size of the Moon and its distance from Earth.

Their figures were quite wrong but were a reasonable effort for people working with the most rudimentary instruments. The Greeks used sundials and water clocks to tell time but did not do much better with them than the Egyptians did. Time remained elusive.

By the third century B.C. the Romans were building the great empire for which they were renowned. In time they took control of Greece, Egypt, and much of the land around the Mediterranean. Like everybody else, the Romans struggled with the ill-coordinated movements of Earth and the Moon, producing a variety of calendars over time, none of which was entirely satisfactory. And the discrepancies were not always accidental. A priestly board charged with adjusting the calendar was deliberately shifting it around to collect more taxes and otherwise benefit themselves. In 63 B.C. Julius Caesar, the most powerful man in Rome, took control of the calendar. He asked advice from one of his Egyptian subjects, Sosigenes, who looked back to an idea that had been devised by Ptolemy. (There were several historical figures of this name.)

With the Egyptian calendar failing to account for the final one-quarter day present in every year, it had been Ptolemy's idea to add an extra day every fourth year. Thus the concept of leap year was born. And in 45 B.C. the so-called Julian calendar with twelve months of thirty or thirty-one days, and a shorter February with a leap day added to it, was put into effect. (The number of days each month had was somewhat different from the present system.) The months were given Roman names—January for the god Janus, March for Mars, the god of war. July was named for Julius Caesar, August for one of his successor emperors, Augustus Caesar. The names for the last four months of the year were taken from the Roman words for the numbers seven, eight, nine, and ten, which at one point

A PORTABLE BRASS SUNDIAL FROM THE ROMAN EMPIRE, FOUND IN THE RUINS OF A GRECO-ROMAN CITY IN PRESENT-DAY TURKEY. A ROD WOULD HAVE BEEN INSERTED INTO THE CENTRAL HOLE TO ACT AS A GNOMON. A TRAVELER FAR FROM HOME WOULD HAVE HAD TO KNOW EXACTLY HOW TO SITUATE THE SUNDIAL FOR HIS OR HER GIVEN LONGITUDE.

these months had been numbered. The Julian calendar would be used for more than 1,600 years.

The Romans, too, used water clocks and sundials to tell time. But despite the considerable advances in math and sciences made by them and the Greeks alike, their time-telling instruments were still rough and inaccurate.

These people were not alone in attempting to measure time. In fact, it is likely that every culture attempted to do so. From about the sixth century B.C. there is evidence in India of the adoption of Babylonian ideas about astronomy and the calendar. The Mayans of Central America divided the year into eighteen months of twenty days each, with a short five-day month at the end. Although the Mayan culture developed long after the civilizations of the Middle East, the Mayans made their discoveries independently.

The Chinese in particular made quite early advances in science. By the third century B.C. they had developed a Neolithic culture with decorative pottery and, eventually, tools and objects made of metal. By the fourteenth century B.C. the Chinese had developed writing and were working in bronze, and in 1361 B.C. they had collected astronomical data about eclipses. At this time they were using gnomons, sundials, and water clocks to tell time, and were dividing the day into twelve equal hours, as the Babylonians had done. They used a year of 365¼ days, understood the cycles of the planets, and would eventually create the first true clock.

An understanding of the heavenly bodies and a concern for the measurement of time, thus, was not unique to the Middle East and Europe. But it was the Europeans who were eventually responsible for ushering in the great revolution in timekeeping.

A PORTION OF A MAYAN MANUSCRIPT INDICATING THE MOVEMENT OF CELESTIAL BODIES. THE MAYAN CALENDAR WAS COMPLICATED AND TOOK ARCHEOLOGISTS MANY YEARS TO DECODE.

During medieval times, farming methods greatly improved. The horses here are wearing collars, which allowed them to draw heavy harrows and plows, making the tilling of the soil more efficient. Nonetheless, change came slowly. The man scattering seed from his apron was using a method that was thousands of years old.

THREE

# The Great Escapement

European culture, after the decline of the Roman Empire, grew conservative and clung to the status quo. For a thousand years after their conversion to Christianity, Europeans retained their traditional lifestyles, which changed only slowly. A peasant working the fields in a French village in A.D. 300 would not have found life much different a thousand years later.

In part, Christianity itself was responsible for this gradual change. According to the Christian church, which was universal to Europe, life was short and precarious, which indeed it was. It had to be seen as a testing ground for entry into Heaven. There was not much point in trying to improve your lot, to get ahead. Instead you should live according to the Christian ethic and thus gain eternal life. But whatever impact Christianity had, the slow alterations experienced in Europe during this time were probably due mainly to the strong tendency of people to continue doing things the way they were raised to do them, rather than looking for an alternate method.

Toward the end of this long period, some improvements were made, many of them seemingly small, but together they set in motion a train of events, the effects of which are with us today. One of these small improvements was the invention of the horse collar. People had known for a long time that an iron plow of a certain design was far more efficient in turning over the soil than the ones they had been using. But it took oxen to draw this iron plow through the earth. At the time, standard harnesses for horses went around their necks and choked them if they had to pull anything heavy. The horse collar shifted the weight to the shoulders. More efficient designs for iron plows soon followed. Farmers began to cut down forests and drain swamps to cultivate more land. In A.D. 900 the horseshoe was greatly improved, sparing horses injury. Increased plowing capacity allowed farmers to rotate three crops instead of two. Productivity improved by 50 percent.

These apparently small innovations resulted in a substantial increase in food production. A larger food supply meant better-fed mothers, healthier babies, well-nourished children who had a greater chance of surviving childhood illnesses, and stronger and more energetic adults. After A.D. 1000 the European population boomed until the Black Death of 1347–1350 reduced it temporarily.

Some of these additional people spread eastward into what is now Poland, Russia, and the Balkans. But many of them began to migrate into towns and cities, most of them still relatively small. Cities expanded, towns grew into urban centers. Cities and industry grew in tandem. People living in cities, where there is little land for growing grain and pasturing sheep and cows, needed jobs in shops and factories. Factories in turn needed a good supply of labor within commuting distance, which in those days meant reasonable walking distance. Old industries began to expand, and new industries arose. Glass, iron tools and equipment, cloth, and other products came to be made in factories employing several workers, rather than in homes and small workshops.

At the same time, there came an upsurge of learning. In the late ninth century a French monk named Gerbert, later to be Pope Sylvester II, studied in Spain, portions of which had been conquered by Muslims. At the time, the scientists and philosophers of Islam were well ahead of what the more cultivated Muslims thought of as the barbaric Europeans. Gerbert learned about the Arabic numerals (the ones we use now), which were far better for doing math than Roman numerals. He also found the abacus, or counting board, which made rapid calculation of large numbers possible—

Prior to about A.D. 1100, the Muslim world had made great advances in mathematics and the sciences. This painting shows an Arabic intellectual outside of Baghdad in what is now Iraq. Literature and the arts were cultivated as well in the Muslim cities of the Middle East.

By the twelfth century, the Europeans were rapidly advancing in the realms of art, technology, and trade. The use of Arabic numerals made calculations much easier, a necessity for money changers, such as the one shown in this painting by Quentin Metsys, who had to rate the relative values of a vast assortment of coins in use in Europe and elsewhere.

a device Europeans had known about but had forgotten. Through the Islamic philosophers Europeans also rediscovered Aristotle, who inspired many Europeans and imbued them with an inquisitive spirit. This intellectual activity flowed everywhere—into astronomy, alchemy (a relative of chemistry), art, and literature. A new institution, the university, began to coalesce in the 1100s, mainly in cities, the foremost of them in Paris. The result was what historians sometimes call the twelfth-century renaissance.

This new learning, especially in mathematics, was a great help to industry. Previously, formulas for making glass or metal compounds would call for "a bit more," or "a medium-sized piece." Greater ease in multiplying and dividing allowed for greater precision in manufacturing. Perhaps more significantly, it spurred the development of the famous double-entry bookkeeping system, which helped merchants determine more accurately what they could afford to pay for wool or had to charge for the cloth from which they made it. Better math was important in working out shares in joint ventures and partnerships, widely used to even and spread out the risks of investment in the precarious overseas trade.

Trade and manufacturing inevitably boomed. It was, in fact, the start of the capitalistic economic system that, for better or worse, is dominant today. To be sure, only a minority of people were involved in commerce, and a small minority at that. The bulk of Europeans were still farmers, in many cases serfs, living a traditional country life tied to the sun and the weather. But commerce was growing in importance. Cities, becoming rich, began to flex their muscles. They raised their own armies and sometimes navies, and to a substantial degree threw off the authority of dukes and princes who ostensibly had power over them. Venice and Florence in Italy were the first of these important city-states, but others were burgeoning, too: Le Mans and St. Quentin in France, Bruges and Ghent in Flanders, Lubeck and Hamburg in Germany, London in England. Craft guilds and merchant associations were formed and became locally powerful. City life grew rich and varied, foreshadowing the great renaissance of 1450 to 1600. After stagnating for a thousand years, music, art, and literature blossomed. The newly rich built splendid homes furnished with cloth, glassware, and furniture shipped from foreign lands. Poverty, disease, murder, and crime experienced an unfortunate growth spurt as well. But Europe was moving forward.

This new industrial factory system needed accurate ways of measuring time. Workers had to be assembled and discharged at specific hours so that factories could run smoothly. Busy merchants had a constant round of appointments with buyers, sellers, and town officials. The town officials themselves had committee meetings to attend. There was an increasing sense that time was money, especially among the merchants. An Italian businessman of the period wrote, "After all, one can catch up with sleeping, eating, and the like on the morrow, but not business. . . . He who knows how not to waste time can do just about anything; and he who knows to make use of time, he will be lord of whatever he wants." That line could have been spoken by an American corporate executive today.

Knowing the time was becoming increasingly important in the twelfth and thirteenth centuries. But systems for measuring it remained poor. Still in use were the water clocks and sundials, which remained as accurate as they were in ancient days. Candle clocks, which marked the hours as they burned down, were sometimes used, but the rate of burning depended on atmospheric conditions, and the candle might be blown out by a breeze through an opened door. Rough rules of thumb were often used instead of precise moments. People might be expected to arrive at work "when it was light enough for a person's face to be seen" at a given distance. A meeting would start "after the early mass." A piece of metal to make a dagger should be heated "for the length of time it takes to say a *pater noster* (a Catholic devotion)." The burgeoning commercial system needed much better timekeeping systems.

Yet, although much of the drive for good clocks would come from the world of commerce, the initial push came from the Roman Catholic Church. The medieval church was a huge and various institution, which extended into most aspects of European life. It has been estimated that at times a third of Europeans were employed by the Catholic Church as priests, monks, and nuns; as artisans constructing churches, cathedrals, and monasteries; as ordinary laborers hired to tend gardens and cattle; and as many other kinds of functionaries, ranging from elegant dignitaries in Rome to clerks shivering in stone monastic cells copying sacred texts.

A central part of the church was comprised of a number of orders—that is to say, brotherhoods and sisterhoods of monks and nuns organized for certain purposes. Some of these orders were dedicated to good works, some to proselytizing among the non-Christians to bring people into the church, and some to prayer. Among the earliest and most important of these brotherhoods was the Benedictine Order, which operated many monasteries spread throughout Europe and eventually other lands.

The Benedictine monks had to till their fields and herd their flocks to make their livings, but their primary function was to offer a carefully worked-out sequence of prayers. Most of these prayers were given during the day, but some had to be offered at night. These prayers did not have to be exactly timed: in medieval days people tended to think in large segments of time, such as "late morning," or "just before sunset," rather than "eleven A.M." or "five-thirty P.M." However, the sequence had to be followed, which as a practical matter meant that each prayer had to be started close to a specified time. For example, the prayer for the ninth hour, which as measured from sunrise was about three in the afternoon, was called none. It began to slide forward until it was coming at midday, and thus our word *noon*.

The Benedictines, like most Europeans of the time, used the system of unequal hours, which had been passed down from the ancient civilizations to Rome and to Greece. As Christianity spread throughout Europe, it brought this system of time with it. As in the past, day and night were each divided into twelve hours, each growing longer and shorter with the seasons. The Benedictines could judge the time fairly well from the progress of the Sun across the sky during the day; and a monk well trained in astronomy could roughly figure the time at night from the movement of the stars. But that was only if the skies were clear, which in places such as England and Ireland frequently were not. It also meant that the monk on call at night had to stay awake in order to rouse the other monks for the night prayer.

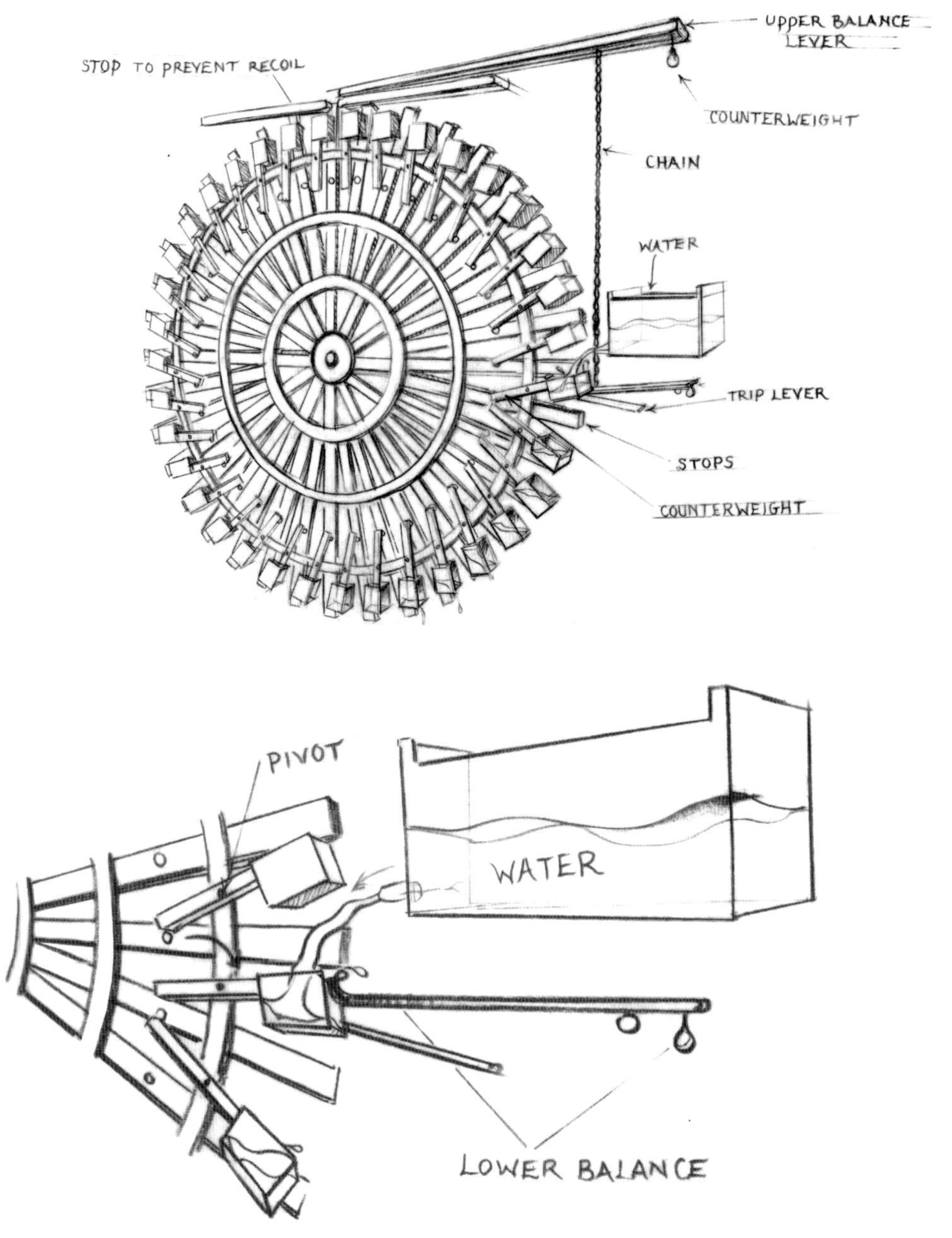


The legendary Su Sung clock was powered by water. It poured into a little wooden bucket, which would pivot downward. The motion would then trip a lever. The lever is attached to a chain, which releases a catch so the wheel can revolve. In the final step, as the wheel swings around, the bucket empties and the catch stops the wheel until the bucket is filled again. In this system the wheel continues to turn in short, evenly spaced steps.

A RECENT MODEL OF THE SU SUNG ESCAPEMENT MECHANISM, WHICH WORKED BY WATERPOWER. THE ORIGINAL MACHINE, WHICH WAS THE SIZE OF A SMALL BUILDING, FELL APART A THOUSAND YEARS AGO, BUT HISTORIANS HAVE BEEN ABLE TO RECONSTRUCT IT FROM DESCRIPTIONS OF IT FOUND IN CHINESE MANUSCRIPTS.

With water and candle clocks among the few, yet unreliable, options for timekeeping, the need for an accurate device grew especially acute. The answers were found in one of the key inventions in human history, the clock escapement. This revolutionary device was ingenious, although its workings are difficult to grasp instantly without seeing it in action. But an escapement of sorts had already been created approximately 200 years earlier. In the eleventh century a Chinese king had ordered the construction of a great astronomical clock that would indicate the motions of the heavenly bodies. He chose to direct this task to a diplomat called Su Sung, who gathered a team of craftsmen and astronomers, and in eight years they had created a clock, driven by water, with an escapement mechanism. Yet, however wondrous this mechanical marvel seemed to the Chinese of the day, they let it fall into disrepair, and it was forgotten for centuries.

It would be the Europeans who would return to and further the use of the escapement. Life in the monasteries and elsewhere, especially the cities, was regulated by bells. Bells sounded regularly from churches, town halls, manor houses, and factories. At times in cities several bells would peal at once. It seemed to many that there was always a bell ringing somewhere within earshot.

Although we cannot be sure, historians generally believe that the escapement mechanism was worked out to ring a bell. It was not too difficult to think of a way to make a bell strike once by some automatic mechanism, but a single bong was not always certain to awaken a snoozing monk. What was wanted was a repeated ringing. And somewhere in the years toward the end of the 1200s a mechanism for striking a bell repeatedly was devised.

We do not know the identity of the genius who invented the clock escapement. Nor do we know exactly when it happened. The best guess puts it between roughly 1270 and 1290. Here, in any case, was how it worked. A fairly large roller was set in some sort of supporting pivot so that it could turn freely. A long rope or cord was wrapped around the roller, and a weight was attached to the cord. Let go of the weight, and it would pull the rope down, spinning the roller.

But of course, according to the laws of motion, the falling weight would accelerate rapidly, and even a long cord would unwind in a matter of seconds. Such a mechanism could be attached to a bell hammer, but it would produce a rapid machine-gun fire of rings and then stop. There had to be a way of holding the weight back so it dropped only a little at a time.

The answer was the escapement. This first escapement depended upon the fact that the top and bottom of a wheel move in opposite directions—that is, when the top is moving to the right, the bottom is moving to the left. With the new system, the weighted roller turned a toothed wheel, called a crown wheel, because it vaguely resembled a crown of those days.

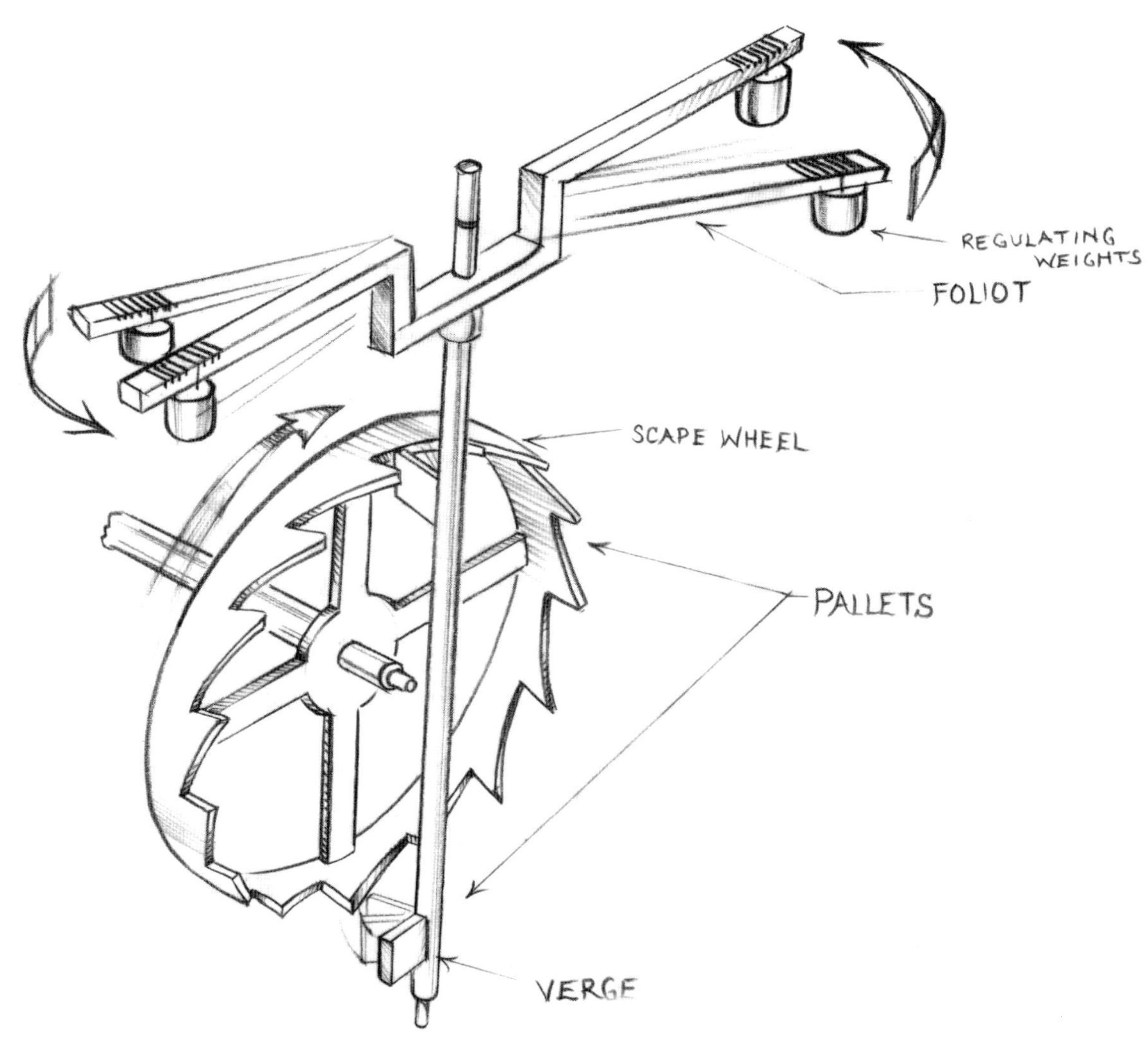


HIS IS THE VERGE-AND-FOLIOT ESCAPEMENT OUT OF WHICH THE CLOCK MECHANISM DEVELOPED. THE CROWN, OR SCAPE, HEEL IS TURNED BY A WEIGHT HANGING FROM A ROPE, WHICH IS NOT DEPICTED IN THE ILLUSTRATION. POSITIONED CLOSE O THE WHEEL IS A ROD, CALLED THE VERGE, WHICH HAS TABS, OR PALLETS, ATTACHED AT TOP AND BOTTOM. THEY ARE LACED SO THAT THEY MESH WITH THE CROWN WHEEL. AS THE WHEEL TURNS, A TOOTH STRIKES ONE OF THE PALLETS, IN HIS CASE THE TOP ONE. THE WHEEL IS MOMENTARILY STOPPED BY THE FORCE OF THE IMPACT, BUT THE WEIGHT CAUSES IT O MOVE AGAIN, PUSHING BACK THE PALLET IN THE PROCESS. THE BOTTOM PALLET THEN SWINGS FORWARD TO STRIKE ONE F THE LOWER TEETH IN THE WHEEL, ONCE AGAIN BRIEFLY HALTING THE WHEEL'S PROGRESS. THE VERGE SWINGS BACK AND ORTH, BRIEFLY STOPPING THE WHEEL EACH TIME AND PRODUCING THAT FAMILIAR TICKTOCK SOUND. THE ARM AT THE TOP F THE MECHANISM, CALLED THE FOLIOT, PROPELS THE MOVEMENT OF THE VERGE AND PALLETS. THE WEIGHTS AT THE ENDS F THE ARM CAN BE SLID FARTHER OUT OR IN TO REGULATE THE SPEED OF THE ESCAPEMENT.

Set in pivots close to the crown wheel was a rod or a staff called a verge. Attached to the top and bottom of the verge, like little flags or tabs, were two pallets [illegible] at approximately right angles to each other. Set into motion, one [illegible] would swing into the teeth, striking one, and momentarily [illegible] jarring it enough to throw it back just a little. However, [illegible] wheel, driven by the weighted rope, would quickly [illegible] pallet and push it back out of the way. This [illegible] pallet into the teeth, once again striking and [illegible]. And so it went, the verge moving to and fro, [illegible] mechanism for a brief moment, to produce the end[illegible]ate with an old-fashioned clock. The system ingen[illegible] the crown wheel to drive it.

The new escapement mechanism, by repeatedly halting the crown wheel, was now breaking time into a stream of small divisions that could be counted: tick, tock, tick, tock, tick, tock. The weight was never allowed to accelerate, but fell for a very short distance at a relatively slow speed and then was halted. (In theory, of course, the weight accelerates fractionally each time it drops, but the amount of acceleration is quite small.)

There was more to this system, however. At some point, possibly at first, whoever devised the verge-and-crown-wheel escapement searched for a way to adjust its speed. They found it in the foliot. This was simply a bar or rod running horizontally across the verge. A weight was attached to each arm of the foliot in such a way that it could be slid back and forth. According to the laws of motion, the farther out the weights were on the arms, the slower the mechanism would move. Thus, the speed of the machine could be varied up to a point.

Though historians believe that the verge-and-foliot escapement was devised at first to ring a bell for several minutes or longer, in all probability the bell hammer was not attached directly to the mechanism, but was hooked into it by means of gears. Gears are a system of trading speed for power, or the other way around. A small wheel with ten teeth geared into a big wheel with a hundred teeth will only move the big wheel a tenth of the way around, while the little wheel makes a complete revolution. The speed

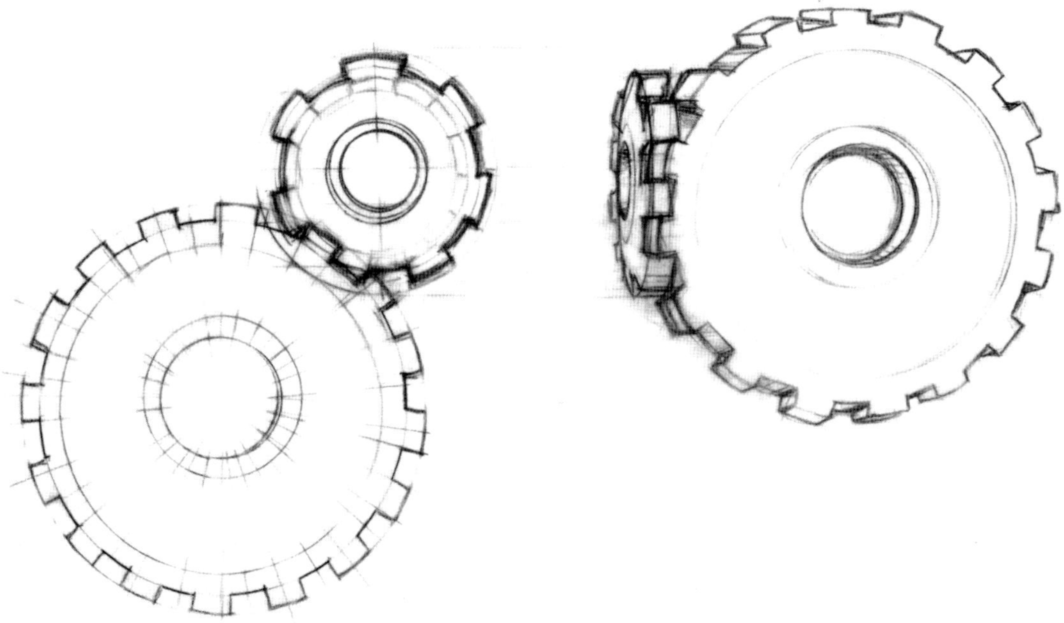

THE LARGER WHEEL HAS MORE THAN TWICE AS MANY TEETH, OR COGS, AS THE SMALL ONE. AS A RESULT, THE SMALLER WHEEL MUST REVOLVE MORE THAN TWO TIMES TO TURN THE LARGER ONE ONCE. THE SMALL WHEEL PIVOTS ON ITS AXIS MUCH FASTER THAN THE LARGE WHEEL. IN EXCHANGE, THE BIG WHEEL MOVES WITH MORE POWER. GEARS CAN BE USED TO CHANGE SPEED INTO POWER AND VICE VERSA. THE ILLUSTRATION TO THE RIGHT SHOWS HOW GEARS CAN TRANSLATE HORIZONTAL MOTION INTO VERTICAL MOTION. THIS WAS NECESSARY IN WINDMILLS AND WATER MILLS, WHICH HAD UPRIGHT WHEELS, WHILE THE MILLSTONES LAY FLAT.

of the big wheel is much slower, but moves with correspondingly greater force: a person turning a crank handle on the small wheel will be able to move an object attached to the big wheel that would otherwise be far too heavy to budge. All sorts of lifts and hoists work on this basis. Reverse the system, and the big wheel will drive the small wheel at a high speed, but with far less power.

By the 1200s Europeans had been using water and windmills to grind grain, pump water, and do other tasks for some time. By the eleventh century, England alone had more than 5,000 mills of various sorts. A water wheel, driven by a rushing stream, would move at considerable speed. However, to grind corn it had to move a very heavy millstone, which might weigh several tons. Gears were needed to transform the speed of the waterwheel (or wind vane) into enough power to turn the millstone, however slowly.

The Wells Clock, built for Wells Cathedral in England in 1392. The verge-and-foliot escapement was eventually replaced by a pendulum, but the complex system of gears is still functioning and rings the bells regularly in London's Science Museum. The clockworks shown here stands 4 feet (1.2 m) high, but the works had to be placed considerably higher in order to allow for the long weighted rope.

Gears performed another function in mills. A waterwheel, for example, was necessarily upright—perpendicular to the ground. A millstone, however, lay flat. The gears could be set up at right angles to each other, to transform vertical into horizontal motion.

Inevitably, the first builders of the new mechanism used sets, or "trains," of gears to ring a bell. Very quickly, however, people saw that the verge-and-foliot system could be used to do a great many other things: ring several bells at various times; run planetarium systems showing the motion of the Sun, the Moon, and planets; make wooden angels pop out of boxes and pop back in again at given intervals. Most importantly, they saw that the machinery could be geared in such a way that it rang bells regularly, as for example on each hour. Clocks had become mechanized.

The hundred years from about 1290 to the end of the next century saw a great boom in clock making. These clocks at first did not have hands, but instead sounded bells. When hands appeared during the 1300s, it was only a single hour hand which revolved around the dial.

These original clocks were huge. For one thing, they had to be high enough to allow the weighted rope a long drop. This meant that they had to be installed in church steeples, city-hall turrets, and towers specially built for them. Secondly, the machinery, with its escapement, ropes, rollers, and gear trains, was complex and large simply because clock makers lacked the skills to work with precision on the scale required for small clocks. Some of these original clocks had wheels a yard in diameter and took up what amounted to whole rooms. The oldest surviving turret clocks from this period are one from 1389 in Rouen, France, one from 1388 in the cathedral in Salisbury, England, and one from 1392, originally in Wells Cathedral, but now in the Science Museum in London, where it can be seen in action. (However, its original verge-and-foliot escapement was replaced with a pendulum in about 1670.)

In these big turret clocks, the crown wheel, although repeatedly halted, still moved at a fairly rapid pace. The speed had to be slowed by gears, which left the mechanism producing a considerable amount of power. Clock makers then began using the excess power to run all sorts of fanciful devices. In addition to the bells, and eventually a clock hand, parades of figures of monks, saints, and angels marched out one door and in another at certain hours. In Norwich, England, in the early 1320s, a clock was built with a dial, a set of tuned bells, and figures of parading monks. In Paris the three wise men proceeded out of a clock in existence since 1326. St. Paul's Cathedral in London had an angel that turned. A clock in Cambrai, France, displayed a calendar. In Strasbourg, France, a clock had a rooster that flapped its wings. These clocks took months to build, often employing experts brought in from distant places, and cost a lot of money. Churches believed the money was well spent if a fanciful clock attracted attention and brought in worshipers. For the towns and cities, it was a matter of civic pride: a wealthy city insisted on having the most astonishing turret clock it could provide.

However astonishing, these turret clocks did not keep very good time. In the fourteenth century nobody understood what shape to make gear teeth in order to produce the least friction. A lot of oil had to be used on the clockworks. Oil thickened and thinned with temperature changes. Worse, it collected dirt and dust, which wore down gear teeth and pivot holes, and when it got thick enough, clogged everything, drastically slowing the clock. Frequently the churches, princes, and town officials who had built these clocks discovered that they needed a full-time employee to maintain, wind, and reset them as needed, which might be every day.

But despite the problems, the turret clocks were considered little short of miraculous by incredulous townspeople who came to stare at them in wonderment as bells rang and roosters flapped their wings, apparently of their own accord. They could not understand how the thing could run by itself.

As a consequence, through the fourteenth century, despite the upheavals caused by the devastating mid-century plague, the so-called Black

Death, a mania for clocks spread over Europe. As early as 1336, when the boom in clocks was just beginning, the city of Milan, Italy, had a clock that sounded twenty-four hours a day, one stroke for one o'clock, two for two, all the way up to twenty-four, which must have made sleep difficult for those who lived nearby. Padua had a similar clock in 1344. Italy seems to have been in the forefront in clock making, but by 1404 the device had spread as far east as Russia.

By 1400 a revolution was complete: Europeans had learned to tell time. Before 1300 time had been an ambiguous thing, passing by invisibly at night and on dark days, leaving people as uncertain of where they were in the day as a sailor in a fog. Now Europeans knew how many hours they had yet to sleep if they awoke when the clock was striking or how long it would be until it was time to quit work or break for the noontime meal. It was a momentous change.

There were practical advantages, too. Astronomers benefited, for they could now time celestial events better and thus make more accurate charts of the movement of heavenly bodies. Mill owners were able to time manufacturing processes more accurately. Whereas previously they had only rough guides, such as that ash and sand for making glass should be heated for "a day and a night," they could now specify 23 hours, or even 23¼ hours. Appointments could be made more precisely and met more promptly. Merchants wasted less time than they had before waiting for each other at meeting places.

Perhaps most significantly, both employers and employees began to think in terms of a fixed working day. On farms in the countryside, the working day was generally tied to a given task. A cowherd or milkmaid had to stick with the job until the cows were rounded up, brought to the barn, and milked, no matter how long it took. Haying, which had to be done in dry weather, might go on until midnight if it was threatening to rain. Conversely, in the dead of winter, workers might slack off a good deal, simply because there was nothing urgent to do. In truth, in 1400 that was still the case for the majority of human beings who were still tied to farm work and the tending of the land.

But for a small but growing minority, the length of the work day was a matter of great importance. Employers wanted to be sure that their workers got to work on time and stayed at their tasks for the agreed number of hours. Employees, in their turn, wanted to be sure they worked only the right number of hours and got the breaks they were supposed to have. Now that public clocks were within sight, or at least earshot, both employers and employees knew where they stood. No longer was a worker expected to be at his bench when it was "light enough to see a man's face at thirty feet," or some other such arbitrary or ill-defined time. People were to work by the clock. The idea of an hourly wage had not yet developed. But during the fourteenth century the notion of paying for overtime, or docking wages for hours lost, was quickly being instituted. From there it would be only a step to the hourly wage, although that would be a while in coming.

Still, employees were hired to work for a set number of hours, frequently shorter shifts for hard jobs such as mining. The hours might be set by bargaining between employer and employee or by town officials. People were now thinking in terms of hours, instead of days.

A second major effect of the sudden—in historical terms—appearance of the clock throughout Europe was the disappearance of the old unequal hours. It was possible to readjust clocks to hours of different lengths by changing the size of the weight, or shifting the smaller weights on the foliot arms. But it was difficult to do so with much accuracy, and in any case, the changing length of night and day through the seasons made the whole process even more complicated. The inevitable result was that the old system of unequal hours was quickly abandoned. It was phased out in Germany by 1330 when clocks were still a novel idea, and extinguished in France in 1370 when Charles V required all clocks in Paris to follow the one in his palace. The idea that night and day were two different states, at least in Europe, had begun slowly to erode.

Perhaps most important of all, Europeans began to be time conscious in a way they had never been before. Among merchants in particular, but with others as well, there was a growing sense that time was a commodity that should not be wasted. Although it has not been thoroughly studied, undoubtedly the clock and the new time consciousness made for an efficiency, at least in commerce and industry, that had not previously existed. How much difference that made in increasing the wealth of Europe would be hard to measure, but undoubtedly it mattered. Time had arrived.

A set of sandglasses made in Italy in the seventeenth century. Each glass has a somewhat different amount of material in it, so that the set could be used to measure four different lengths of time.

FOUR

# Springs and Pendulums

By 1400, then, virtually all towns in Europe had at least one public turret clock. Cities had several of them, and even a small village might have one in its church steeple. Most Europeans, by that time, had grown up knowing how to tell time. It had always been part of their lives.

Inevitably, people began wishing to have clocks of their own at home. There were several practical reasons for this. A clock would help in cooking. It would let you know when the maidservant had been gone too long at the market and was probably up to no good, or it would tell you when it was time to get dressed for church or to leave for an appointment. But practicality was only part of it; human vanity was involved, too. Just as today people buy expensive cars often to impress their family and friends, so a few people began installing clocks in their homes.

The turret clock, however, was too large for most homes. At first only princes and earls had space enough for a clock and could afford to build one. So one answer to the desire for a home timepiece turned out to be something very simple: what we call the hourglass, or sandglass. We might think that the sandglass goes far back into ancient history, but it actually was developed around the time that turret clocks were first being built. Sandglasses, which in fact used some fine dustlike material such as powdered egg shell, could be made to signal quite accurately the passage of smaller portions of time—a few minutes, an hour, a few hours—simply by adding or subtracting some of the substance it used. (Of course you had to time it initially against something, such as a sundial, a clock, or another sandglass.)

But the sandglass signaled a return to the old principle of using the flow of something to measure the passage of time. It suffered from one basic problem: while a sandglass could tell you when five minutes, a half hour, or two hours had passed, it was not easy to use one to judge the time in between, when it had only partially completed its flow. That is, you could not tell very well from an hourglass when twenty minutes had elapsed, much less thirteen minutes, or thirty-three.

What was needed, then, were smaller clocks. Once again we are not sure who first made them or when they appeared, for none of these early small clocks has survived. At least one historian believes that small clocks were made at the same time as the big turret clocks, but the general opinion is that they came later, probably after 1400.

Artisans took on the challenge and discovered it was quite possible to build small weight-driven clocks. A small weight might not have much driving force, but the smaller mechanism would not need much. The bigger problem was working with much smaller tolerances and such a reduced scale. For one thing, the iron of the day contained impurities, which made a certain amount of roughness inevitable. Brass was a better metal for the purpose, but even with brass, working to small tolerances was difficult. An error of 1/16 inch (1.6 mm) in a gear wheel 2 feet (61 cm) in diameter might not be critical; in a wheel 2 inches (5 cm) in diameter it would be disastrous. But by the early 1400s the most skillful clock makers were beginning to learn how to work in small dimensions.

There was, however, a second problem with small weight-driven clocks. They were not truly portable in the sense that you could use them to tell the time while you were traveling in a coach or ship, for the motion of travel, especially in a storm at sea or on a rough mountain road, would disturb the even unspooling of the cord. A different sort of power was needed.

In fact, an alternate power source already existed. It was the coil spring, the sort of mechanism that powered windup toys until fairly recently, when battery-operated toys became standard. A coil spring, however, had one built-in drawback: the power lessened as the spring wound down, and the clock would eventually slow. The solution was another device already in existence, the fusee wheel. A fusee was shaped like a cone. A cord was attached to the end of the spring and wrapped around the fusee, starting at the wide bottom end. It thus unwound from the top first. The trick lay in the fact that, as with gear wheels, it took more power to move a small wheel than a large one. Therefore, when the cord was first unwinding from the narrow top end of the fusee, it required greater power than it did as it wound farther down the cone. The gradual loss of power in the spring was thus equalized by the gradually lessening amount of power needed to turn the fusee. The fusee was attached to the clock mechanism by gears or a shaft, and the usual escape-

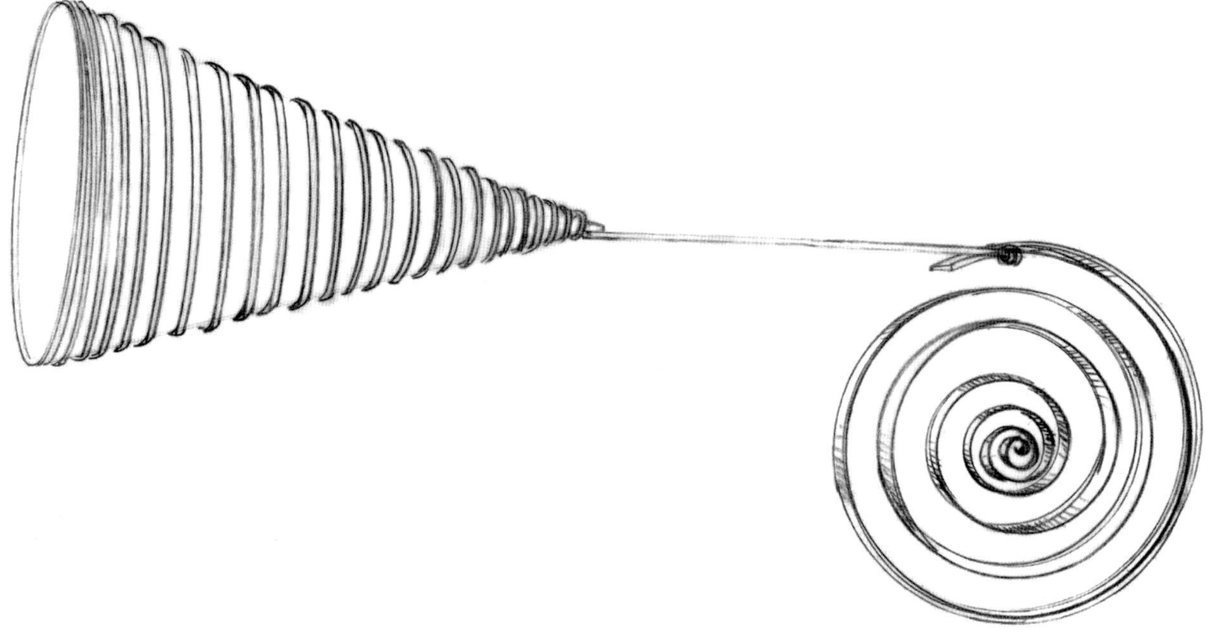

THE FUSEE OPERATES ON A PRINCIPLE SIMILAR TO THE ONE AT WORK IN THE GEAR SYSTEM. THE SPRING PULLS ON THE CORD, UNWINDING IT AND TURNING THE CONE-SHAPED FUSEE. AS WITH GEARS, MORE POWER IS NEEDED TO TURN THE SMALLER END THAN THE LARGER ONE. THUS, AS THE UNWINDING SPRING LOSES POWER, IT IS STILL ABLE TO MOVE THE FUSEE, BECAUSE IT TURNS IT FROM A LARGER CIRCUMFERENCE AND LESS POWER IS NEEDED.

THE HAND SHOWN HERE IS PART OF A PORTRAIT OF A SIXTEENTH-CENTURY GENTLEMAN. THE IMPORTANCE OF TIMEPIECES AS ITEMS OF PRESTIGE IS SUGGESTED BY HIS CHOOSING TO BE PAINTED AS HE HOLDS OUT HIS WATCH FOR DISPLAY.

ment forced the spring to uncoil in short steps, a bit at a time. Spring power began to replace weight power, except in large clocks.

Needless to say, these small clocks, filled with gears with tiny teeth and even tinier hand-cut screws, required a great deal of painstaking work to make and thus were expensive. Not surprisingly, the earliest spring-and-fusee clock on record belonged to a French king, Philip the Good. It dates from 1430, by which time, in all probability, the rich and powerful were beginning to have clocks in their mansions and palaces.

By the 1500s the demand for small, portable timepieces had become a craze among the rich. There was a scramble to see how small a clock could be made. By the 1500s they were getting small enough to be carried about, usually pinned or tied to the clothes. Even that was not small enough, though. Some were made so tiny that they could be set in the handle of a dagger or into a finger ring. Queen Elizabeth I of England had a tiny ring watch with a little arm that scratched her finger like an alarm at specified times. These tiny clocks—or as we would say today, watches—were not very accurate, but that hardly mattered because they were mainly objects of conspicuous consumption, display pieces meant to excite curiosity and envy.

The passion for clocks ran not only to miniaturization. In the 1500s, princes, kings, and wealthy merchants demanded fanciful table clocks with which to impress the visitors to their palaces. Some of these clocks approached the level of art in their design and ornamentation and can be seen in museums today. Not only were they encrusted with jewels, inlay, and gold, they had mechanized displays. One famous clock rested in a small ship carrying a Turkish warrior, two rowers, and a monkey perched on the prow, all sitting on an elaborate base. The eyes of the warrior would move from side to side and at certain moments he would raise his arm and the oarsmen would start to row. A similar clock sat on the back of a bronze elephant whose eyes also moved. Other table clocks had dials on all sides showing the movements of various celestial bodies. Still others were built to resemble grand castles.

Watches, too, became highly ornamented. By the 1600s dials were being decorated, and watch backs were painted with miniature portraits or little religious or domestic scenes. (These were, we must understand, not

THIS SIXTEENTH-CENTURY CLOCK WAS IN FACT A FANCIFUL SHOWPIECE MADE FOR A RICH FAMILY. WHEN ACTIVATED, THE OSTRICH MOVED ITS NECK, AND THE BEAR BEGAN TO BEAT ON THE DRUM. SUCH CLOCKS TODAY ARE RARE AND VALUABLE MUSEUM PIECES.

wristwatches, which did not develop until much later, but flat, round pocket watches, usually with a cover that could be opened to reveal the dial.) Among the wealthy, owning a watch was all the rage. By the 1600s personal timepieces had become cheaper, and the small but growing middle class of merchants, lawyers, and bankers now owned them. Laborers still depended on the town clock or even the church bells.

However handsome these clocks and watches were, accurate they were not. There were limits to what even the most skillful clock maker could produce with his hands, especially given the less refined metals of the day. Beyond mechanical problems, there was also the fact that different localities set the time as it suited the local lord or church authorities. Some started numbering the hours at sunrise, some at sunset, others at noon or midnight. Some used a twenty-four hour system, which was a problem for striking clocks. Others used the current system of two sets of twelve hours for each day. As a traveler moved from east to west any distance, say from Warsaw, Poland, to Paris, France, sunrise would come slightly later each day, and the time in the cities the traveler was passing through was correspondingly different. It would be some while before a uniform time system was established, and in the meantime merchants and travelers had to struggle with a patchwork of time schemes in the lands where they did business.

Despite the advances, the demand for ever more accurate timepieces remained. For one thing, reliable clocks would improve navigation on the open seas, which helped save lives, ships, and goods. For another, given the growing sense that time was a valuable commodity that should not be wasted, business owners and workers would feel pressed to use that time more productively. For a third, astronomers were almost totally dependent on time measurement to make accurate charts of the movement of the stars. Not merely seconds, but fractions of seconds, counted. In turn, accurate navigational charts and general calendars also depended on a sound knowledge of astronomy.

Astronomers struggled. One of them, Bernard Walther from Nuremburg, Germany, achieved better accuracy by counting the number of teeth in a clock wheel that passed a given joint. Another famous astronomer, the Dane Tycho Brahe, used a clock with a wheel more than a meter (3.3 feet) in diameter, which had a thousand teeth. By 1563 Brahe was able to measure time down to a few minutes, and in 1587 he had it down to four seconds. But Brahe had, besides clocks, a specialized type of clepsydra using mercury, which did not change its flow as readily as water. The best clocks we know of from that time were said to vary no more than a minute per day, which meant they might be off several seconds each hour. Most clocks did not perform so well however. Watches might be off a half hour per day, clocks a quarter of an hour.

In the centuries leading up to the late 1600s, advancements in the production of more accurate timepieces came mainly in small increments, from the development of better materials and the improved skills of clock makers to produce ever more uniform, tightly meshing gear trains. The principle of the clock still remained the same: a weighted rope or coil spring, interrupted by a verge-and-foliot escapement in a stop-and-go fashion, drove a gear train which in turn moved a hand or hands around a dial, rang bells, and performed various types of displays. The minute hand became standard.

But then in the 1600s came a dramatic new way of making clocks. It probably began in the 1630s, when the great Italian scientist Galileo Galilei was sitting in church and watching the lamps hanging on long chains from the ceiling, swaying slightly back and forth. It seemed to him that no matter how large an arc each lamp made—that is, how far it swung from side to side—it took the lamp the same time to make the brief journey. This was contrary to common sense. Surely a swinging object will take longer to travel a long distance than a short one? But when Galileo tested his observation, he discovered it to be correct.

The explanation lies in the fact that a weight swinging on a cord is actually falling (and then of course rising again as it completes its arc). Therefore, according to the laws of motion, it accelerates on the downward swing, so that a weight with a longer arc will be going faster as it reaches bottom than a weight with a shorter arc. It is also moving faster as it starts to rise.

The greater speed exactly compensates for the longer arc. No matter how far a given weight on a given cord travels, its travel time will be the same.

What makes the difference, Galileo discovered, is the length of the cord: the longer the cord, the longer the period, or amount, of time it takes to complete a full arc. Galileo very quickly saw that a swinging weight, or pendulum, might be harnessed to a timekeeper. In 1637 he drew a design for a pendulum clock, but he never got around to building one, or otherwise developing the idea.

Then in 1656 the Dutch scientific genius Christian Huygens, unaware of Galileo's design, built a pendulum clock. There has been a little controversy over who should get credit for the invention, but generally historians give it to Huygens, especially as his design was better in certain respects than Galileo's plan.

The basic idea of the pendulum clock was that the pendulum would time the movement of the escapement. The pendulum, of course, would soon run down, as you can see by swinging a weight or bob from a string. So the back-and-forth movement of the escapement, controlled by the pendulum, was used to give the pendulum a slight tap at each swing to keep it in motion. However, the venerable verge-and-foliot escapement,

This model of Galileo's pendulum design was built at a much later date using the diagrams he recorded in his notebooks. The unvarying back-and-forth movement of the bob at the end of the pendulum rod regulated the movement of the clock-works. However, the Huygens design had some advantages over Galileo's and was the starting point for the pendulum clocks that followed.

which had served clock makers well for nearly four centuries, was not suited to the pendulum.

Huygens tried various methods to get around the problem, but the solution eventually came from someone else, probably either Robert Hooke or William Clement, both English, possibly in the years from 1666 to 1671. This was the anchor escapement, so called because of its shape. The swing of its back-and-forth motion was much shorter than the swing of the verge and foliot, which had to make something close to a 90-degree turn. This allowed the pendulum to make a shorter arc, which added to its technical accuracy. The old verge and foliot was rendered somewhat obsolete, but it did not disappear entirely and was occasionally used for special designs or purposes.

At about the same time, perhaps in 1675, Huygens devised another important device: the balance spring. (Once again there were arguments over who should be given credit for the invention.) In this system, the balance wheel was attached to the balance spring so that it wound the spring a little as it turned. The balance spring would then, when wound tightly enough, spring back, reversing the motion of the balance wheel. The balance wheel was in turn driven by a mainspring, which, like any watch mainspring, had to be wound by hand from time to time. As we shall soon see, pendulum clocks could not be used aboard ships and were thus of no use in navigation. The balance system was able to avoid this problem.

Over the next hundred years or so, clock makers improved pendulum clocks to the point where, by the eighteenth century, there were pendulum clocks beating once a second that would vary no more than ten seconds a day. Eventually there were pendulums up to 13 feet (4 m) long, which took two seconds to beat, such as the one made for the Greenwich Observatory on the outskirts of London. Astronomers now had a tool with which they could make much finer determinations of celestial movements than ever before. This, in the long run, was no small matter, for without the advances in our understanding of the universe made possible by accurate timepieces, space vehicles and probes could not have been developed.

Another advance in clock making involved the use of jewels as bearings. The various wheels and escapements turned on axles or pins, which in turn were set into pivot holes. Oil was used to reduce the friction of the axle or pin turning in the pivot hole, but oil, as we have seen, collected dust, which would grind away at both the pin and the walls of the pivot hold and eventually clog the mechanism. At the beginning of the eighteenth century, a Genevan and two Frenchmen working in London decided to use jewels, generally harder than metal, in the pivot holes. They decided that rubies had the ideal hardness. They learned how to drill tiny pivot holes in the jewels and to set them in the watches. Not everyone agreed that the new jeweled watches were an improvement on the old system of well-oiled brass pivot holes. But by the 1720s jeweled watches were being made, and by the nineteenth century all fine watches were jeweled.

Improved clocks allowed astronomers to make better calculations of the movements of celestial bodies. These in turn led them to realize that the Julian calendar was gradually falling behind. Here a medieval astronomer makes measurements of the heavens with what was advanced equipment for the time.

FIVE

# Setting the Year Straight

Europeans first worked out the calendar that most of the rest of the world uses today. In 45 B.C. Julius Caesar adopted the Julian calendar with its year of 365 days and one additional leap day every fourth year, to make a year of 365¼ days. But in fact, the year is not quite 365¼ days, but about 11 minutes 14 seconds short of it. The Julian calendar was thus fractionally longer than the actual solar year, and right from the beginning began to fall slightly behind—that is to say, after a while the real summer solstice was coming a day or more before the calendar claimed it would occur. For ordinary purposes, the slippage did not matter much: over the course of an average lifetime there might be a slippage of a quarter of a day.

But by the late Middle Ages, this small discrepancy had added up to ten days. Once again this was not critical for most human activities. The slippage was so slow that people easily adjusted to the change and by the 1500s were doing things in late March that had once been done in early April.

But this slippage, however small, mattered a great deal to the Roman Catholic Church. By this time the Church was under growing attack from reformers, who felt that the Church had become too rich and too concerned with worldly matters, such as power politics, at the expense of its religious mission. This movement was the Reformation, out of

The crucifixion and resurrection of Jesus Christ are powerful images central to Christianity. They were painted countless times from the medieval period on and celebrated with great musical works. Fixing the right date for these holy events was a matter of prime importance for the church.

which the Protestant churches grew. Nonetheless, the Roman Catholic Church was still a powerful institution in Europe and increasingly in European colonies in the Americas and elsewhere.

Particularly critical to the church was the celebration of Easter, which at the time was a more important holy time than Christmas has become. Easter was a "moveable feast," which was supposed to fall on "the first Sunday after the full moon occurring on or after the vernal equinox." Many other dates important to the church were tied to Easter, such as Good Friday and Lent.

To the Roman Catholic Church, the dates of the crucifixion and resurrection of Jesus Christ were sacred matters. They were not arbitrary in the way that the American Thanksgiving is arbitrary, fixed by law and custom to a convenient date roughly close to the original event it celebrates. The church could not simply shift Easter Sunday around as it desired. It had instead to discover when the crucifixion and resurrection took place and celebrate them on those dates. To do anything else would be sacrilegious.

In the sixteenth century, the calendar slippage was well known to astronomers and philosophers. Indeed, as early as the thirteenth century, an English genius named Roger Bacon had written a paper on the problem. But for one reason or another, through the years the popes had never gotten around to doing anything about it.

By the 1500s the whole thing had become a scandal. Many people—astronomers, church fathers, princes—were urging the popes of the day to take action. Finally Gregory XIII, who had become pope in 1572, decided to undertake the necessary calendar reform. He turned to an astronomer named Christopher Clavius, who got advice from another astronomer named Luigi Lilio. They had two tasks before them. One was to work out a system that would keep the calendar in line with the natural solar year. The second was to adjust the Julian calendar then in use so that its vernal equinox fell on the date the equinox actually occurred.

The first problem was solved by making a minor adjustment in the Julian calendar. The 365-day year, with a leap year every fourth year, would continue as before. However, leap year would be skipped once a century, on the century year, for example 1700, 1900, and so forth. But even this shift did not quite add up, so a second provision was made: leap year would be observed on any century year divisible by four hundred, for example 1600, 2000, and so forth. That is the system we use now: no leap years on years ending with 00, except those divisible by 400, which is why our grandparents and great-grandparents had no leap year in 1900, but we had one in 2000. Even this system is not quite perfect, for it loses a day roughly every 2,000 years; but it is assumed that by that time whoever is around can add an extra day in somewhere, if the present calendar system is still in use.

For Pope Gregory's team, figuring out a proper calendar was the easy part. It would be more than 120 years before a leap year was skipped in 1700, and nobody then alive, or indeed their grandchildren, would be affected. But dropping days out of the current year to make the calendar accurate would affect people then alive considerably. The plan was to eliminate ten days out of the year to bring the calendar in line with the solar year. Therefore Pope Gregory issued a bull, or edict, which said that October 4, 1582, would be immediately followed by October 15, thus cutting ten days from the calendar.

Instantly a great many people expressed their alarm. What was supposed to happen about debts or taxes due to be paid on one of the missing days? Would they be due on October 4, October 15, or never? Some people even began claiming that they did not have to repay a debt due on one of the missing days until the next year.

Then there were superstitious people who felt that somehow they were being cheated out of ten days of their lives. Suppose they had a birthday on one of the missing days—how old would they be? Would they have somehow lost a year? In fact, what about birthdays in general? Any given date now was no longer an exact number of years from the same, original date. Was a person born on June 15 thus supposed to celebrate his or her birthday on June 15, or on June 25, which was the original June 15? Not until everybody who was alive when the new

FRANCISCVS

IN QVORVM

**A manuscript for the reform of the calendar ordered by Pope Gregory XIII and signed by him**

Martin Luther was one of the most important figures in the development of the Protestant churches that came out of the Reformation. Many Protestants were hostile to the Roman Catholic Church and for this reason refused to have anything to do with the reformed Gregorian calendar.

calendar was put into effect had died would the birthday problem straighten itself out.

A more serious problem was a religious issue. By 1582 the Reformation was in full force. Many people, indeed entire nations, such as England, had broken with the Roman Catholic Church and joined one or another of the new Protestant churches. To many of these people the pope was the enemy—even, in the eyes of some, the Antichrist. Such people flatly refused to accept an order from the pope, even when it was as sensible as reforming the old Julian calendar to bring it in line with the motions of Earth.

And finally, there were plenty of people of a conservative nature who simply did not embrace change. The old calendar had been good enough for their fathers and mothers, and it would be good enough for them.

The net result was that the new Gregorian calendar was adopted only slowly. The English and the Germans did not adopt it until the eighteenth century. The American colonies, under English rule, adopted the Gregorian calendar when the English did in 1752. Japan accepted it in 1873, Russia at the time of its revolution in 1917, and China after the communist takeover in 1949. It is the calendar the world recognizes today. However, some religious groups, such as Muslims and Jews, have their own religious calendars, which they use to set their holy days.

The Gregorian calendar, despite the fact that it is in step with the true solar year, is not, in the view of many, entirely satisfactory. The number of days in each month is arbitrary and makes little sense. For example, August has thirty-one days because Caesar Augustus didn't want his month to be shorter than July, Julius Caesar's month. Furthermore, the days of the week fall on different days of the month year after year—that is, January 1 is not always a Sunday, but travels through the week in a disorderly fashion, due in part to the leap days.

There are other problems. Many businesses operate their finances on a quarterly basis. They issue reports of earnings every three months and pay dividends to stockholders each quarter. Governments, too, issue reports about the health of the economy and other matters on a quarterly basis, and self-employed people are expected to pay their taxes four times a year. But the first quarter of the year, from January 1 through March 31, has 90 days (91 in a leap year), the second quarter has 91, and the last two quarters have 92 days. The last two quarters are slightly longer than the first two, a fact that must either be ignored or adjusted for in making business payments and reports.

Not surprisingly, a number of calendar reforms have been proposed. Probably the best known and most widely accepted is one worked out in 1834 by the Roman Catholic priest Marco Mastrofini. Under his system, the year is divided into four quarters of ninety-one days each. Each quarter has a month of thirty-one days followed by two months of thirty days. Ninety-one divides evenly by seven, so that the days of the week would always fall on the same date. That is, if it were decided that the year should begin on Sunday, January 1 would always be Sunday, year after year; March 31 would always be Saturday, and so forth. This adds up to 364 days, so a World Day would be added between December 30 and January 1. (Under this system there would of course be no December 31.) And there would be a leap day, as usual, except that it would come every fourth year after June 30. To keep the days of the week aligned with the dates of the month, the extra days—World Day and leap day—would not be assigned any other name. It would be strange at first to have days that were not Wednesday, Monday, or anything else; but undoubtedly people would get used to it, and no doubt would not mind the extra holiday every year.

According to this system, the Fourth of July would always be a Wednesday, which would probably mean that workers would never get a three-day weekend, but Thanksgiving would probably always come on November 23, so the traditional four-day holiday then would continue as always. Would we like knowing that our birthday would always fall on, say, Thursday, and never on a weekend? Maybe. Maybe not.

This world calendar, as it has been called, has many supporters. Books have been written about it, organizations have been founded to promote it, and resolutions have been sent to the United Nations urging its adoption. It has never been officially accepted. For one thing, some religious groups, including Orthodox Jews and some Christians, believe that the seven-day weekly cycle is sacred and should not be broken up by extra days. A greater difficulty is that a calendar change of this kind would require a massive conversion of account books, airplane schedules, school years, tax rolls, and countless other records. And of course there would be again the birthday problem. The author's own birthday, June 27, would now fall on June 26. Which would be the right one to follow? (However, in fact, on leap years everybody whose birthday comes after February is a day off.) There are, thus, a lot of people opposed for various reasons to altering the present calendar system. Will it ever be put through? Your guess is as good as anybody's.

By the 1500s European ships were sailing everywhere across the globe in search of trade goods and frequently outright plunder. European cities, especially ports such as Venice, Genoa, London, and Lisbon, were becoming rich and powerful through trade. Their bustling harbors were the focus of the newfound wealth and importance of nations such as Spain, Portugal, Italy, England, and France.

SIX

# Navigation Time

The commercial mercantile system of trade growing rapidly in Europe in the late Middle Ages and Renaissance was making more than a few people well off and some of them quite rich. This mercantile system depended on water-borne freight, traveling on rivers, the seas, or the ever-expanding canal systems linking European cities. Overland shipping was then difficult and dangerous. European roads—indeed most roads anywhere—were little more than ruts running through fields and forests. In summer they were as hard and rough as a plowed field. In winter they turned into bogs of mud into which carriage wheels would sink to the hubs. In spring heavy rains turned small streams into raging torrents that could sweep away roads, sometimes drowning travelers when their carriages were capsized in floods. Also there were always highway robbers to worry about. Snow, fallen trees, landslides, and mountains were just more of the challenges of overland travel.

So, people and freight moved mostly by water. Even though the sea passage between Venice and Naples, for example, was far longer than the overland route, it might often be quicker, depending on wind and weather, to go by sea. Furthermore, even the relatively small ships of those days could carry more cargo in their holds than could a wagon, or even a train of several wagons.

Ocean trade developed rapidly, and by 1400 Europeans were beginning to make long trips through often snarling seas. At first the Portuguese, under their famous Prince Henry the Navigator, led the way. They began traveling from Lisbon down the west coast of Africa. In 1488 they rounded the Cape of Good Hope at the southern tip of Africa and by the early 1500s had established trading bases in China, India, and various places in Southeast Asia. In 1492 Columbus, driven to prove that he could reach "the Indies" by sailing west, bumped into what became known as the Americas. The Spanish, who had sponsored Columbus, quickly took advantage of the opening and rapidly built up their sea trade, especially with Mexico and Central America.

Soon thereafter the English, French, Dutch, and other nations joined in. At first these European seamen and the kings and queens who supported them were looking for raw materials that would bring large profits in Europe—spices from the East Indies, where Indonesia is now, silks and porcelain from China, timber and furs from North America, and gold from Central and South America. Soon, however, they began to establish colonies in many places, conquering the local people, in some cases enslaving them, and where they could, simply taking what they wanted, as the Spanish did in Mexico and Central America. Not everybody was easily conquered, though. Many African tribes remained independent, while the Chinese and Japanese proved to be resistant to the Europeans. In such cases the Europeans would trade with the locals in the standard way.

The rewards from this overseas trade could be enormous. A lucky investor could make a fortune from a single trip. But the risks were huge as well. Vessels were wrecked in storms, taking millions in goods and dozens of men to the bottom. Competing nations sometimes attacked each other's vessels. Hostile peoples murdered landing parties in search of food and water.

One of the greatest difficulties was navigation: how did you get from one place to another across thousands of miles of trackless sea? This was hardly a new problem: the Greek, Roman, and other armies fighting over the lands around the Mediterranean often had to cross a lot of open water. The Norsemen in the Middle Ages traveling to Greenland, North America, the British Isles, and other places also sometimes had to sail out of sight of land. To some extent the captains of such ships had learned to navigate by the Sun and stars. In the Northern Hemisphere there were certain "fixed" stars that did not appear to move, especially the Pole Star, which indicated north. Through the years astronomers had developed a good understanding of the motion of the stars. However, figuring out your position by the stars was not easy, especially given the poor, or indeed nonexistent, maps of the time.

As a consequence, most sea captains navigated by instinct and experience. They could determine their speed by throwing overboard a log attached to a rope with equally spaced knots on it, then seeing how long it took the rope to play out to its full length. With a compass they knew, at least roughly, the direction they had been traveling, and combining speed and direction they could determine approximately how far they had traveled from their position on the previous day.

The system was clearly in need of improvement. A ship would not hold a steady course for any length of time, and captains were never sure if they had gotten the previous day's position right. Errors only accumulated.

To make matters worse, a three-day storm could drive a ship hundreds of miles off course, leaving the captain with no idea where he was. He would then be forced to reckon by the Sun and the stars as best he could. Again and again ships in such a predicament wandered helplessly across empty seas while food and water dwindled, and the sailors grew weak, sickened, and died. In other instances errors in navigation would bring ships into hostile territory or toward unknown, rocky coasts.

Everybody knew there was a better way to navigate, if only someone could figure out how to do it. As far back as Grecian times, maps of many areas had been drafted. Mapmakers had begun to add horizontal and vertical gridlines to their maps. These gridlines could be numbered so that navigators could specify any point on the map by the numbers of the horizontal and vertical gridlines that intersected there.

These gridlines became known as lines of latitude and longitude, and eventually they were extended to reach around the globe. The latitudinal lines are the ones that circle the earth horizontally—that is, running east and west. They are parallel to each other and are big near the equator, growing smaller as they move towards the poles.

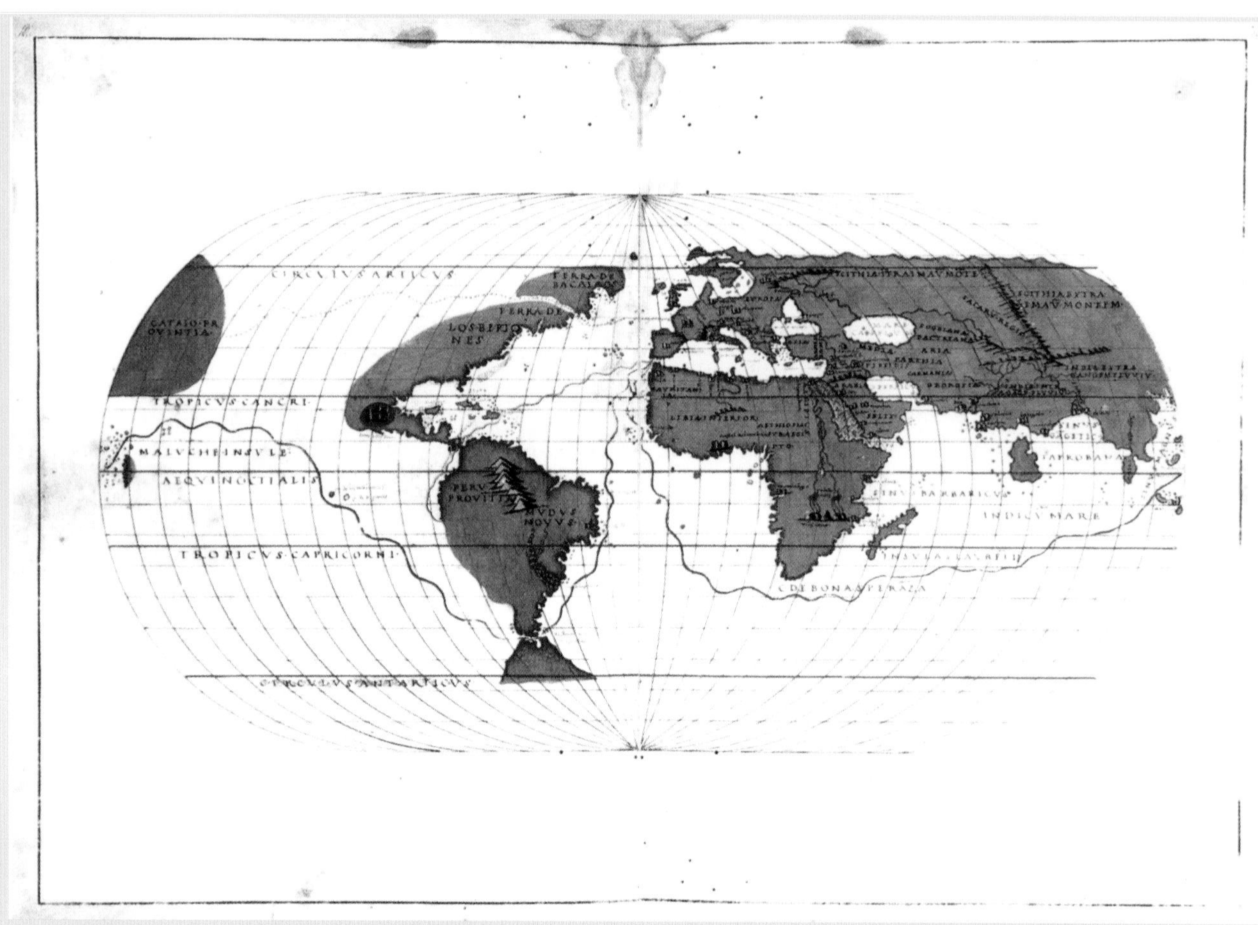


**This map, dated about 1536, shows vertical lines of longitude and the horizontal lines of latitude, although not quite the same as the modern system. In the early days of exploration, Europeans were unsure about the exact shape of the globe's landmasses. North America is particularly distorted; even into the seventeenth century Europeans believed that North America was much narrower than it is. As a result, when English rulers gave pieces of land in future Virginia and Massachusetts to colonists, they often drew the property lines all the way to the Pacific Ocean, which they thought to be only a few hundred miles from the Atlantic.**

Longitudinal lines are drawn somewhat differently. Instead of being parallel, they all pass through both poles. They are thus the same size. The distance between these lines is stated in degrees: there are 360 degrees around the world, a number that goes all the way back to Sumerian times. A trip of 180 degrees of longitude will take you exactly halfway around the world. Degrees are subdivided into 60 minutes per degree, 60 seconds per minute, familiar numbers that suggest how closely linked time and navigation are. At the equator a degree is about 68 miles (109 km).

With the advent of this new system, mapmaking gradually improved. A great step forward was made by Gerhardus Mercator, a Flemish cartographer. The problem he set out to solve was how to translate a map on a globe onto a flat piece of paper. It is not an easy task. Making a flat map of a relatively small piece of the globe, say the size of a city or a small state, works fairly well, because there is not much of a curve to it. It is the larger pieces that can cause problems.

Mercator's solution was to draw a map in which lines of longitude and latitude were kept exact, passing through the same points that they did on the globe. At the equator, a flat map will appear as it does on the globe. However, as you proceed toward the poles, the areas will be increasingly distorted, until the point is reached at the far north and south—as for example in northern Canada—where the landmasses appear several times larger than they actually are. But for navigators, the great advantage was that on a Mercator projection, latitude and longitude are correct, so that a sea captain trying to make a certain landfall could be sure of its position.

By the 1500s, then, there were maps available to seamen with reasonably accurate lines of latitude and longitude drawn on them. Today, for example, the city of New Orleans lies just about at the intersection of thirty degrees north latitude, ninety degrees west longitude. That is all very well; but how, then, in a vast empty sea, do you find the position of your ship?

As it worked out, latitude was relatively easy to determine at sea. The Sun, of course, changes its course through the seasons. In the Northern

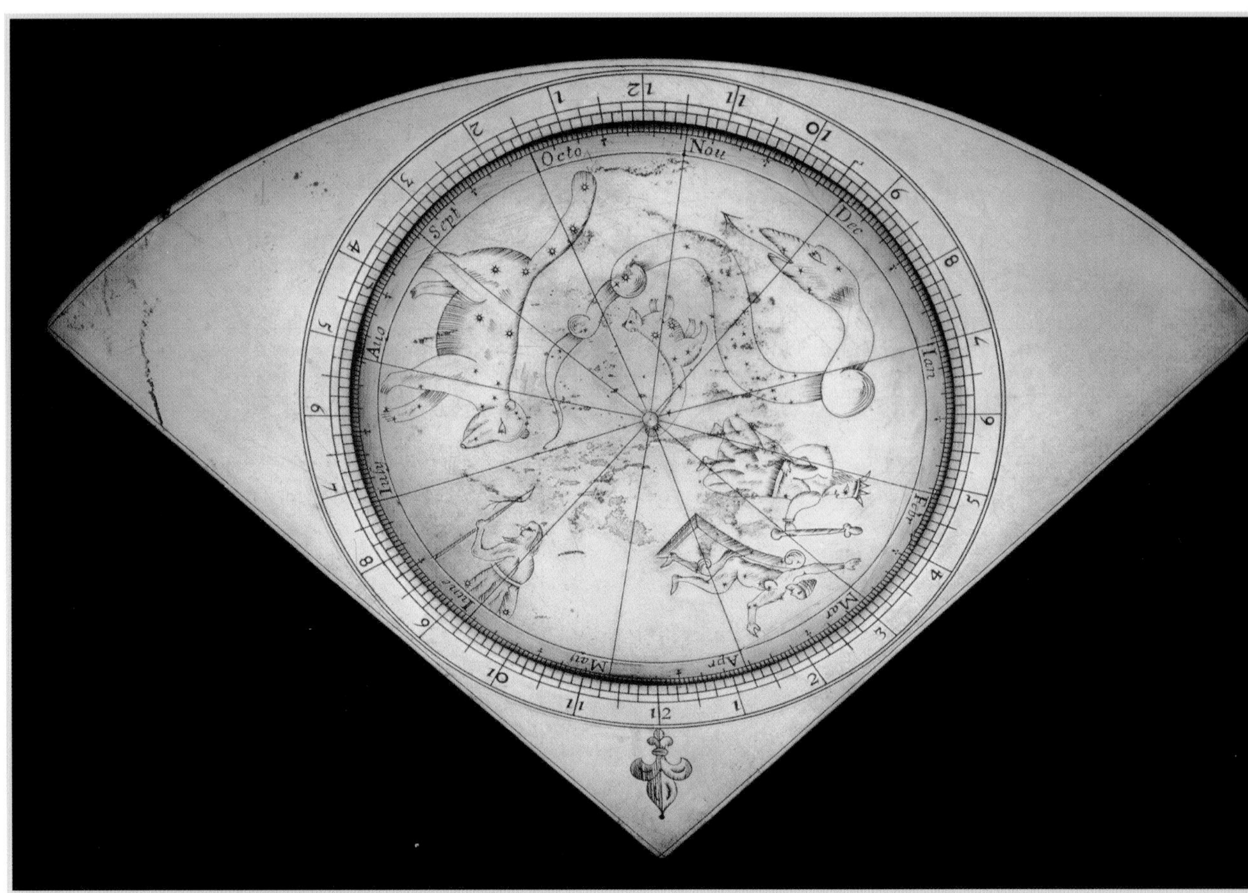


**Over time, fairly complex instruments, such as this quadrant, were developed to help in navigation. Such devices improved captains' abilities to determine their positons at sea. Still, there remained great room for error.**

Hemisphere it travels fairly high in the sky during the summer months, low in the sky during the winter. The farther north you go, the lower the Sun will appear to travel. The key point is that the position of the Sun at noon—or any specified hour—will always be the same for a given date at a given latitude. That is to say, at thirty degrees north latitude the Sun will appear to be in the same place in the sky when it is noon in New Orleans, or when it is noon at some point farther east in the Atlantic Ocean. Given this fact, astronomers were able to work out charts giving the position of the Sun at noon, or other hours, at each latitude for every day of the year. It was painstaking work, and the results filled a book with many pages, but the principle was simple enough.

To determine the angle of the Sun above the horizon, the navigator on board used a pair of sticks or rods hinged together at one end. He aimed one stick at the horizon, raised the other stick until it pointed at the Sun, and measured the angle formed by the two sticks. He could then look through his charts until he found the date and the angle, and from that read his latitude. Making this measurement on a rocking ship was not always easy, but an experienced mariner would repeat the measurement a few times and then calculate an average. Over time, instruments for measuring the angle of the Sun vastly improved. Results were surprisingly good. Mariners learned that the safest, if not the shortest, way to cross thousands of miles of open ocean was to head directly for the latitude of their destination and sail along that latitude until they got to where they wanted to go.

But finding your longitude at sea was a far more difficult matter. In theory there was a way to do it. Let us suppose that when it is noon on a ship in the Atlantic, it is six o'clock in the evening back at the home port of London. That means that the Sun above the ship has traveled six hours since it crossed London when it was noon there. Six hours is a quarter of a day, which means that the Sun has made a quarter of its trip around the world, or 90 degrees (360 degrees divided by 4). All the navigator needs to do, then, is to find the longitude 90 degrees west of London, which would put him about at New Orleans (or St. Louis, depending on his latitude).

This was a neat and simple system. There was only one problem. There was no way of being sure what time it was back at the home port. Even by 1700 the marvelous new clocks that had been developed did not work with sufficient accuracy on board and often did not work at all. For one thing, the motion of a ship would hopelessly derange a pendulum. For another, continual changes of temperature and air pressure, which were inevitable on a ship traveling a southerly route to go around the tip of South America or Africa to reach the Pacific, would regularly alter the speed of any clock or watch. These errors, however small, would add up day by day. At the latitudes where European ships frequently crossed the Atlantic to get to the Americas, an error of a minute on the clock might be worth 50 miles (80 km) of longitude. A five-minute error, then, would leave a captain well off his course, and a clock that had been at sea for a month might easily be an hour ahead or behind.

By 1600, when Spanish and Portuguese were hauling great wealth from Central and South America, this fact was well known. In 1598 the Spanish king Philip III offered a substantial prize to anyone who could find a way to determine longitude at sea. The losses of treasure ships would make even a huge award well worth the money.

Many schemes were proposed. The best of them involved navigating by the stars. Methods of celestial navigation had been worked out, but they were complicated, time consuming, and in any case were no good when the stars could not be seen because of bad weather. In most instances sea captains continued to judge longitude by guesswork and observation.

By 1700 England was growing especially concerned. A relatively small island nation, it could grow wealthy only through trade. To that end, it was beginning to build a colonial empire, which would eventually grow to become the most extensive of all. Finding a way to determine longitude at sea was critically important, not just to England's merchant vessels, but to its navy as well, for a strong navy was essential to keeping control of the colonies. In 1714 the British Parliament offered an award of 20,000 pounds—equal to millions of dollars today—for a solution to the longitude problem.

By the sixteenth century, Europeans, especially the Spanish conquistadores, were taking over substantial portions of the New World. In this picture Spanish troops, with the advantage of metal swords, armor, horses, and guns, battle Indians. In part the Spanish justified their conquest of Central and South America by calling it an effort to Christianize "heathen" peoples. Catholic missionaries, such as the one holding the cross at right, were often brought along for that purpose.

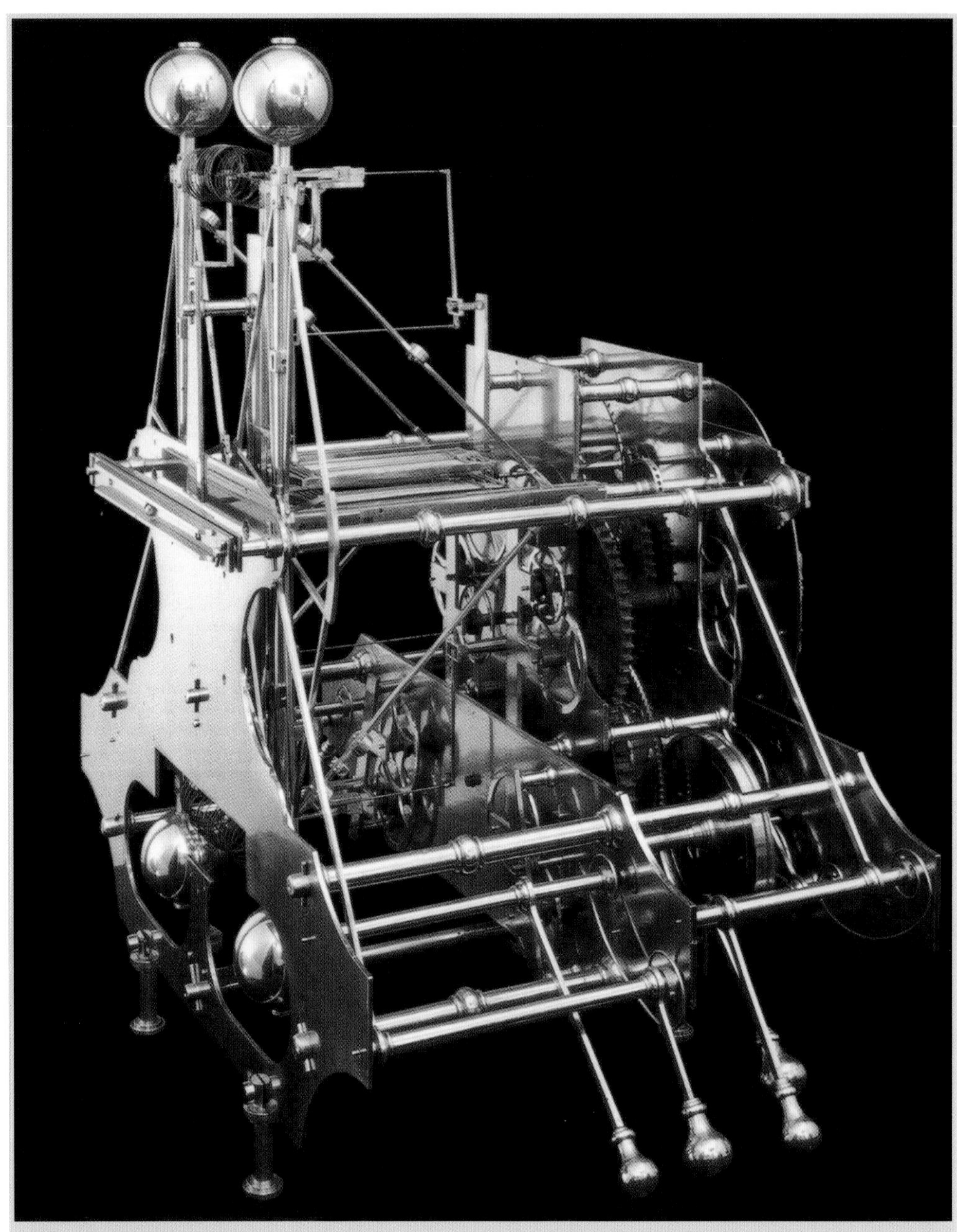

Harrison's first navigational clock, dated 1737, was a very complex piece of machinery—far too complicated to explain in a few words. However, it was the best navigational instrument ever built to that time, although Harrison would soon build others that surpassed it.

Various people set out to claim the prize. Among them was a young man named John Harrison, born in 1693, the son of a carpenter and caretaker of an estate. As a boy Harrison was possessed of immense curiosity about how things worked. His parents could not afford to send him to school, so he studied on his own, reading what books on science he could get hold of. Before he was twenty, he had built an excellent pendulum clock. In 1722 he built a turret clock for a local squire that was made entirely of wood so it would not rust. That clock has been running ever since.

By 1727 Harrison was building clocks of great accuracy. Often he worked with his brother James, although there is no doubt which of the two was the genius. Again and again he worked out new ways to solve old problems. He built a pendulum with a kind of grid made of various metals with different rates of expansion, which would stabilize the temperature changes and neither expand nor contract. He devised a new kind of escapement as well, called the grasshopper escapement, because it appeared to kick like grasshopper legs. Although he did not develop them, he applied roller bearings to clock pivots, and he experimented with devices made by Huygens and subsequently forgotten. Some of his clocks were so accurate that they varied by no more than a second a month. They were, one historian says, the most accurate clocks to be made until the late nineteenth century.

In 1730 Harrison decided to go to London to get financial support from the Board of Longitude for an effort to develop a clock that would keep accurate time on ships. The board was headed by Edmund Halley, discoverer of Halley's Comet. Besides Halley, the Board of Longitude included other astronomers and was strongly biased toward a celestial solution to the problem of longitude. However, Halley met with Harrison and was impressed by his drawings. He sent him to see George Graham, then England's leading clock maker. Harrison was worried that Graham might steal his ideas, but he had no choice. In one of the most celebrated meetings in the history of timekeeping, Harrison went to see Graham at ten o'clock in the morning, and they were still talking at eight that evening.

An early clock made almost entirely of wood by John Harrison. Wood did not, of course, rust as iron did. If properly cared for, it could last for hundreds of years. This one, built in 1715, still works.

Graham, too, was deeply impressed by Harrison and his ideas. He lent Harrison some money to get him started. For five years, Harrison worked to create a clock known today as Harrison's Number 1, or simply H-1. It is an odd-looking contraption, measuring 3 feet (1 meter) in each dimension. Many of the wheels were made of wood. It used rollers, the grasshopper escapement, and was driven by springs instead of a pendulum.

Harrison and his brother James tested the clock on a local river and then brought it to London to show to Graham. He was impressed and sent Harrison to the Royal Society, the main English scientific body, which was also enthusiastic about the timepiece. To win the 20,000-pound prize, though, a navigation system had to be accurate within half a degree of longitude on a run to the West Indies, equal to about 34 miles (55 km). Thirty-four miles was a fair margin of error, but undoubtedly the British government felt it would be lucky to get that close. The West Indies, islands in the Caribbean, were chosen because England had important colonies there.

It took a year to arrange the trial, and then it was on a run to Lisbon, Portugal, instead of the West Indies. Why this decision was made is not clear. In any case, the clock worked. As the ship was returning to England, the captain concluded that the land they had spotted was a certain point jutting into the sea. Harrison's clock told him that the captain was wrong by about 60 miles (100 km). Again Harrison and his clock were right.

But instead of demanding a trial on the West Indies run, Harrison told the Board of Longitude that he wanted to improve his clock, in addition to making it smaller. He asked for some money to support his continued efforts. With this he built Harrison 2. This clock was smaller—although actually heavier—and incorporated a number of minor improvements. The board tested it in the laboratory by subjecting it to severe changes of heat and temperature and by shaking it violently. The clock passed those tests "within the nearest limits proposed by Parliament, and probably much nearer."

But the obstinate Harrison was sure he could do better still, and instead of asking for a test run to the West Indies, he went home to make Harrison 3. For reasons never made clear, he spent twenty years making this new clock. From time to time he got money from the Board of Longitude to carry on the work, but funding can hardly be the reason for the long delay. It seems that Harrison was not so much interested in the money as the fame. He wanted to make the perfect timepiece.

Meanwhile, time was flying by. The astronomers were hard at work. In particular, some astronomers associated with the famous Greenwich Observatory on the eastern side of London were attempting to make accurate charts of the movements of the stars and to work out formulas from them by which longitude could be determined. It could be done, at least theoretically, with great accuracy. But there were problems. For one, making measurements of the angles of various stars from the horizon was not easy on a rocking and pitching ship, even with new instruments such as the sextant. For another, the calculations were time consuming. In some cases, calculations had to be made as if the navigator were standing at the center of the earth. To work this out could take several hours. Finally, there was always the problem of weather. Navigation via the stars was no good if the stars were covered in clouds. Nonetheless, many astronomers, and others concerned about navigation, felt strongly that celestial navigation would prove to be the best system.

Harrison finally finished H-3 in 1759. But he had hardly completed it before turning around and starting to build yet another timepiece. The testing of H-3 was delayed because of the so-called Seven Years' War then in progress. (America's French and Indian War was part of the Seven Years' War.) In the meantime, Harrison had gotten a London watchmaker named John Jeffreys to make him a pocket watch, based on Harrison's ideas. The watch proved to be amazingly accurate. Harrison decided to skip testing H-3, so long in the making, and move directly towards making a near-perfect watch, using the ideas he had developed over so many years. The new timepiece had several innovations, including a variation of the old verge-and-foliot escapement. H-4 was only 5 inches (13 cm) in diameter and weighed only 3 pounds (1.4 kg)—big for a pocket watch of course, but very small for a navigational clock.

Harrison had this marvel ready for the board in 1760. Unfortunately, the astronomers and their supporters now dominated the Board of Longitude. They stalled the testing of H-4 (H-3 was to be tested at the same time). Finally, late in 1761, a ship set sail for the West Indies with both H-3 and H-4 aboard. When the ship arrived in Jamaica in January 1762, instruments were set up to establish exact noon. After eighty-one days at sea, H-4 had lost only five seconds, making it far more accurate than the test required.

Harrison's watch had clearly won the award, but jealousies continued. Harrison's fight to gain his due was discouraging. Eventually he appealed to King George III himself, who was interested in science and particularly enthusiastic about clock making. When the king heard the story he said, "By God Harrison, I will have you made right." So finally in 1773, eleven years after the test run to the West Indies, and forty-three years after the famous meeting with George Graham, the London watchmaker John Harrison was granted his prize. He was approaching eighty years of age.

Ironically, Harrison's great timepieces were soon superseded by simpler ones. But Harrison had shown that a clock good enough to navigate by could be made, if problems such as friction and temperature could be addressed. Nonetheless, for some time, solely out of habit, ship captains continued to navigate by celestial movements and even blind guessing. In the end, though, the new system took over. Harrison's clocks, the beginning of it all, are still in the National Maritime Museum in Greenwich, England. Three of them are still running.

# *Greenwich Mean Time*

Despite the accuracy of Harrison's and later marine chronometers, celestial navigation continued to be used for some time. Obviously, in any navigating system, lines of latitude and longitude have to be numbered in some fashion. Latitude has a natural starting point at the equator. That is how we number lines of latitude today: so many degrees, minutes, and seconds north or south of the equator.

Lines of longitude have no similar natural starting point. In numbering them, early mapmakers had a tendency to assign zero degrees of longitude wherever they happened to be. The French put zero at the Paris Observatory, the English at the Greenwich Observatory, and so forth.

As it turned out, some very good star tables were developed in Greenwich around the time Harrison was devising his famous marine clocks. Charts of this kind had to be issued for every year to match changes in star movements. People associated with the Greenwich Observatory began issuing new charts on a regular basis. They became widely used, and out of sheer habit people became accustomed to thinking of zero degrees of longitude, the prime meridian, as running through Greenwich, London. Inevitably, when time zones were established much later, it seemed natural to start at Greenwich. And so today nearly all clocks are set according to Greenwich.

The Greenwich Observatory near the Thames River in London has always been a tourist attraction. The metal line, which the man with the camera is straddling, is the prime meridian, that is, zero degrees of longitude.

Early factories were simple by modern standards. Still, they transformed nineteenth-century life. Here raw cotton is being put through the first of a series of stages that would eventually result in thread or yarn. In turn, the thread would be woven by machine into cloth, eliminating handwork that had been a principal task for women for thousands of years.

SEVEN

# Time for Everybody

For almost five hundred years, from the time the old verge-and-foliot escapement was developed by some anonymous craftsman and the mid-1700s, when John Harrison built his famous H-4 seagoing watch, experimenters of all sorts had been improving the accuracy and convenience of clocks and watches step by step. They have made them smaller, more stylish, even reduced the friction present in the mechanisms. The clocks of the late eighteenth century were certainly accurate enough for everyday purposes. Only astronomers and people doing certain kind of scientific experiments had any need for better systems of time measurement.

But these watches and clocks were expensive. Indeed, many were deliberately built as show pieces with fancy cases, ornamentation, and all sorts of built-in extras, such as planetaria showing the movements of celestial bodies and other moving displays. The less than wealthy certainly did not own watches, and very few people had even simple clocks. They continued to go by the Sun, the Moon, the stars, and the clock and bells set in the local church tower.

And indeed, most had little need for better systems of timekeeping. Through much of the eighteenth century most people in Europe, the Americas, and elsewhere still worked in the countryside tending sheep, making butter, harvesting grain. They needed clocks only to remind them

FOR MOST NINETEENTH-CENTURY MILL WORKERS, LIFE WAS DIFFICULT AND THE WORK HARD. THESE MEN IN A FORGE MAKING METAL INGOTS TOILED IN OFTEN DREADFUL CONDITIONS IN WHICH SERIOUS INJURY OR EVEN DEATH WAS A CONSTANT THREAT. THE HOURS, TOO, WERE GRUELING: A SIXTY-HOUR WEEK WAS NORMAL, AND MANY LABORERS WORKED LONGER.

when it was time to go to church. It was only the small, although growing, middle class living in cities that needed to know exactly what time it was.

But as we have seen again and again, changes to society brought changes to the business of telling time. In the thirteenth century the need to call monks to prayer made an automatic bell-ringer important. In the sixteenth century the Catholic Church's need to fix Easter correctly led to the new ways to measure the year. In the seventeenth century the profits to be had from overseas trading interested people in improving timepieces as navigational aids.

In the mid-eighteenth century one of the most momentous movements in history began. Increasingly people switched from agriculture to manufacturing as a means of earning a living. The so-called Industrial Revolution began in England in roughly 1750 with the invention of machines for making textiles. It moved on to the United States in the early 1800s and at about the same time was spreading across Europe to Russia. Eventually it took hold in Japan, China, and other Asian nations. The Industrial Revolution is today spreading through developing nations such as Thailand, Indonesia, India, and Zaire, where traditional agricultural villages, even hunting-gathering societies, exist within a few miles of vast, teeming, often chaotic cities.

The unfinished Industrial Revolution has, over 250 years, moved hundreds of millions of workers off the farms and into factories, mines, construction sites, railroads, and other industrial centers. It was in part driven by several changes in agriculture. New machinery for harvesting, threshing, and other time-consuming chores, along with new farming methods made it possible for one farmhand in the nineteenth century to do work that required five, ten, even twenty people a century before. The spare workers, often along with their families, drifted into cities, where they found jobs in factories.

At the same time, capitalist entrepreneurs were discovering that great fortunes could be made in machine-made goods. Machine-made cloth, for example, was not only cheaper than the handmade kind, it was better—more uniform and stronger. Farmers' wives, who had for thousands of years spent long, boring hours spinning and weaving, eagerly bought the new machine-made cloth whenever they could afford to do so. The same process was at work in the making of tools, including iron plows, axes, wagon wheels, and hammers. Machines in factories could turn out better products faster and more cheaply than the local blacksmith or the farmer could at home. The Industrial Revolution, thus, was fed by both a growing source of labor and a growing demand for the cheap, new products. It was an upward spiral of production and consumption. Workers busy in factories, especially if they lived in cities, did not have the time or space to spin and weave, to make shoes and spoons. They had to buy these items ready made.

Factories could be built in the countryside, and at first they were, particularly in the early days when they were run by waterpower and had to be set up near streams and rivers. But with the invention of the steam

Early railroad trains resembled the old horse-drawn coaches and hardly traveled any faster. But quickly the system was improved, and by the time of the Civil War, the United States as well as many nations in western Europe were webbed with rail networks that were critically important in building the modern industrial system.

engine, it was more practical to build factories in cities, where ships and river barges met railroad lines and where there was a large number of working people a trolley ride or even walking distance away.

The Industrial Revolution dramatically altered settlement patterns. At the end of the Civil War in 1865, 70 percent of Americans lived on farms or in small towns. By the early years of the twentieth century, only four decades later, the majority of Americans was city dwellers. In 1820, as the Industrial Revolution was just beginning in the United States, New York had a population of 123,000, and Chicago did not exist. A hundred years later New York had more than 5 million people, with Chicago approaching 3 million. It is a process we have seen before, when the horse collar and other agricultural improvements impelled people into the cities, and the mercantile system of business began to bloom. But this time it was not a minority who was affected. It was the majority. Wherever the Industrial Revolution rolled, it changed life for everybody and often in drastic ways. Farming had always been hard work, especially in the days when butter was made in a churn and firewood was split with wedges and a maul. But the chores were varied, and there were slow times in the winter when families could sit inside by the fire and chat while they occupied themselves with small jobs.

In some ways factory work was an improvement. The workers were inside when rain pelted down or temperatures dropped below freezing, when on a farm they might have been outside bringing in the cattle for milking. And there was nothing terribly interesting about spinning yarn all day long in a cold house or hoeing row after row of vegetables. Still, after the novelty had worn off, factory work was, for most people, a deadly routine. The work week was six days, not five as it is today, and the work day in some cases was fourteen hours long, although over time it was reduced to twelve and ten. Workers were also, in most cases, badly underpaid. With a steady stream of workers flowing off the farms, and in some countries such as the United States arriving on ships as immigrants, employers could always find somebody willing to work for the lowest wage. By the late 1800s in the United States, England, France, and other industrialized nations, many industrial workers were making just enough to pay rent on a tiny apartment in a fetid slum and to buy just enough of the cheapest food and clothing to keep their families fed and clothed.

There was, however, a more positive side to the new capitalist industrial system. With the greater efficiency produced by improvements to machines and new inventions such as the railroad and the electric motor, goods became more plentiful and prices for them went down. The standard of living, even for badly paid workers, climbed. Nonetheless, despite the availability of canned food, better, cheaper clothes, and much else, workers and their families were pinched. They resented their bosses and hated their jobs. They formed unions, went on strike, and particularly in Europe, joined socialist organizations whose aim was to give workers a better deal. And all of these matters conspired to make the measurement of time as important to working people as it was for the middle class.

First of all, to function properly, most factory systems need to have most of the workers there. We can see how this works by comparing it with a system that readers are likely to be familiar with, the school. A teacher cannot teach if the students are not in class, and the students cannot learn if the teacher is not there. This means that custodians have to be there to open the school and see that the heat and water are turned on. School bus drivers, crossing guards, administrators, and many others take their place in the order of the day. In the end, schools are run by the minute—one class ends at 10:55, the next begins at 11:05, and so forth. Promptness is essential if a school is to properly function.

So it was with factories as the Industrial Revolution was sweeping across fields and pastures. The employers needed to have the workers there on the dot, and they needed to make sure that the workers gave them the full number of hours they had been hired for. People who lived within a few minutes' walk of the factory might be able to leave home as the factory bell began to strike. But those who lived at any distance had to know when to leave for work so they could arrive on time.

More significantly, for the first time in human history many, if not most, people were working by the clock. It was no longer a question of staying in the fields until the hay was in. In the factory, the job was never done, but went on and on for weeks, months, and years. For both employees and employers, time was, in the exact sense of the word, money.

Not surprisingly, for centuries mill workers had worried that their bosses were shifting the clocks to stretch out the work day. In fact, it was not easy to make daily changes in the works of a turret clock, especially one with a public face. But to those early factory hands, the clock was a mystery that only the boss understood, and they worried. They had always wanted to have clocks they could control themselves, as did the workers of the nineteenth century.

In addition, not only did a given factory have to be run by the clock, but the factory as a whole had to be integrated into a growing and increasingly complex industrial system in which one factory might be dependent on what was happening a thousand miles away. In particular, as the railroads spread across Europe and the United States and then elsewhere during the nineteenth century, they replaced earlier transportation forms, especially the shipping traffic moving up and down rivers, lakes, and canals.

Railroad lines had to run by schedules if they were to work efficiently and profitably. Customers had to know when trains were leaving and arriving. The railroad lines had to know which locomotives and cars would be available when and where. On top of it all, many of these early railroad lines had only a single track. Trains had to be carefully timed so that two going in opposite directions would not suddenly meet, to the detriment of passengers and freight. Factories, then, had to take railroad schedules into account when considering when to bring in raw materials and when to ship finished products.

And there was more to consider. Factories depended upon a steady stream of raw materials, but they had only limited storage space. Goods had to be moved in and out according to a tight timetable. Everything in the system—people, raw materials, finished goods—was linked together. It had to work like, well, clockwork.

So, by the mid-nineteenth century, most people needed to know what time it was on a regular basis. The market for reasonably accurate, inexpensive watches was large and ever growing. Inevitably, manufacturers jumped in to fill the need.

In the seventeenth and early eighteenth centuries, the English were the leading makers of clocks and watches. Their watches were generally superior to others, and they outsold other nations. By the late eighteenth century, the French were challenging the British, but in fact, they were often using parts made by craftsmen of another country, Switzerland. Very rapidly the Swiss forged ahead. Several factors were at work. For one, labor in the Jura, a poor mountainous region, was much cheaper than it was in England and France. For another, the people of this region had high rates of literacy and the ability to work with numbers, in a world where a great many people still did not read or write. These Jura Swiss were a better-educated workforce than most. In addition, in the eighteenth century many French clock and watchmakers fled France for Switzerland to escape religious persecution. By the late eighteenth century, the Swiss were turning out some 85,000 watches a year, a small number by today's standards, but a substantial figure then.

By this time, the Swiss were beginning to mechanize watch manufacturing. From the beginning, clocks and watches had been made by hand, one piece at a time. So, indeed, was nearly everything else. Not until the mid-1700s, when machines for spinning wool into thread and weaving thread into cloth were invented, did the idea of making goods by machine take hold. The key to mass production by machine was the concept of interchangeable parts. Previously, a trigger for a gun or a spring for a clock were each tailor made for a specific gun or clock. With the system of interchangeable parts, all triggers and springs meant for particular models would be identical—or nearly so—and would fit any gun or clock of that model.

It is generally believed that the first system of interchangeable parts was worked out by the American Eli Whitney to make guns for the Ameri-

SEARS, ROEBUCK & CO., (Incorporated), Cheapest Supply House on Earth, Chicago. 459

Clock Department—Continued.

**Java.** No. 62939. Polished Wood Case in imitation of black onyx, fancy gilt engraving, 6 marbleized columns with artistic bronze caps and bases, large fancy bronze side ornaments and feet; height, 11¾ inches; length, 18½ inches; dial, 5½ inches; fine 8 day movement made by the Waterbury Clock Company, strikes hours and half hours on cathedral gong bell, American white dial with Roman figures, or fancy gilt dial with Arabic figures. Price, $6.30.

**Sicily.** No. 62940. Very fancy polished Wood Case, in imitation of black onyx, with elaborate gilt engravings; large fancy bronze handles, feet and moulding; height, 11 inches; length, 17 inches; very fine 8 day movement, made by the Ansonia Clock Company, strikes hours and half hours on cathedral gong bell, fine American sash and dial, with fine visible escapement. Price, $6.90.

**Marble.** No. 62942. Very fancy polished Wood Case, in imitation of brown Italian or verde antique (green) marble top base and columns, with imitation black onyx body; fancy gilt engraving, with fancy gilt bronze ornaments and tops and bases to columns; also heavy bronze side ornaments and feet; length, 17 inches; height, 11¼ inches. The top of the clock is ornamented by beautiful gilt bronze figure of lady and harp; height, 8½ inches; is fitted with fine 8 day movement, made by the Waterbury Clock Company; strikes hours and halves on cathedral gong bell; very fancy gilt dial with Arabic figures in black enamel; has a patent regulator by which the clock can be regulated without touching the pendulum. Price, $8.45.

The above clock is a work of art, and must be seen to be appreciated. It has the appearance of a clock that would sell at from $30 to $40. It is a most beautiful clock, to which we cannot do justice by any description or engravings we could possibly give you.

**Pointer.** No. 62943. Fine bronze ornament for mantle or top of mantel clock; height, 4 inches; length, 7½ inches. Price, 95c.

62943.

**Onyx.** No. 62945. Wood Case, with new process indestructible finish, which is a most excellent imitation of Mexican onyx, and except that it is examined very closely no one would believe that it was not a real onyx clock. It holds a beautiful polish, and with proper care would last a lifetime. If case gets soiled or dirty it can be wiped off with a damp cloth without any fear of injury; has fancy bronze feet, made in artistic scroll designs; fine Corinthian style bronze tops and bases to columns; bronze lions' heads, with rings in mouth, as side ornaments; fancy gilt dial and sash, with black enameled figures; length, 17 inches; height, 11½ inches; has fine 8 day movement, made by the old reliable Seth Thomas Clock Company of Thomaston, Conn., and is fully warranted by them; strikes hours and halves on cathedral gong bell; has patent regulator by which the clock can be regulated without touching the pendulum. If you are in need of a clock, now is your opportunity to have one of the finest in town. If your old clock needs repairs, it will pay you better to discard it and add a little to what the repairs would cost and have a new one. Price, $5.90.

NOTE.—This clock is being sold by retail jewelers and installment houses for $12 and $14.

**Ormonde.** No. 62946. Beautiful bronze figure of horse, for mantel ornament or top of mantel clock; height, 7¾ inches; length, 8 inches. Price, $1.75.

62946.

**Colusa.** No. 62944. Fine polished Wood Case, in imitation of marble, with fancy gilt bronze side ornaments, fancy gilt sash; height, 11¾ inches; length, 10 inches; dial, 5½ inches; fine 8 day movement, made by the Waterbury Clock Company, strikes hours and halves on cathedral gong bell; with American white or gilt dial. Price, $4.50.

62947.

**Ceres.** No. 62947. Fine bronze statue of lady with bundle of wheat and sickle. Makes a beautiful ornament for mantel or top of mantel clock; height, 7 inches; length, 7½ inches. Price, $1.90.

**Tick Tack.** No. 62948. Height, 11 inches; dial, 5 inches, with mahogany finish, one day time only. Price, 70c.

No. 62948¼. Same as above, with alarm. Price, 95c.

62948.

**Knight.** No. 62941. Elaborate gilt bronze case, with very fancy engravings and scroll decorations, ornamented with a fine statue of a bugler; very fancy sash, with fine visible escapement; height, 15 inches; width, 15 inches; has fine 8 day movement; made by the Ansonia Clock Company; strikes hours and halves on beautiful cathedral gong bell. Price, $14.85.

NOTE.—Such a clock as this cannot be found in the average retail store, but is a real work of art, one that you will not find in any other than the finest stores in the large cities. It is a clock that will retail at $25 and upwards. Price, $3.25.

**No charge for boxing or cartage. The prices we quote are for the goods carefully packed and delivered on board the cars in Chicago.**

**Don't overlook our Grocery Department, and make up an order of 100 pounds or more, and thus secure the very lowest tariff rate possible.**

**Marbleized Wood Clocks on this page weigh, boxed, from 15 to 19 lbs.; Bronze Clock, about 40 lbs.; Bronze Ornaments, about 15 lbs.**



BY THE 1890S, INEXPENSIVE CLOCKS WERE BEING SOLD TO ORDINARY FAMILIES EVERYWHERE. THE CLOCKS ADVERTISED IN THIS SEARS, ROEBUCK CATALOG THOUGH OFTEN EXTREMELY ORNATE WERE STILL AFFORDABLE. AT BOTTOM LEFT, THE FANCY CLOCK WITH THE STATUE WAS PRICED AT $14.85, PERHAPS A WEEK'S WAGES AT THE TIME. THE LITTLE CLOCK AT BOTTOM RIGHT WAS SELLING FOR 70 CENTS.

can Revolution. Some historians believe that the Whitney gun parts were not truly interchangeable, but in any case the system was on its way. By the late eighteenth century, the Swiss were using machines that could mass-produce some of the parts for the cheaper kinds of watches. The parts were rough and had to be finished by hand to fit into a particular watch, but it was a significant advance. By the early nineteenth century, one factory was turning out 100,000 cheap watches a year, using a system that was partly mechanized.

The Swiss, too, began using a new type of escapement, the cylinder escapement, which allowed watches to be made thinner and smaller. Hitherto, personal watches had been pinned to the clothing, hung around the neck, or hung from the belt. They were inconvenient and easy to steal—stealing watches was almost an industry in the eighteenth and early nineteenth centuries. Slim watches could be quickly slipped in and out of the pocket and soon became the fashion. In addition, a slim watch did not make a large bulge in the tight-fitting clothes fashionable during that period.

Between the Swiss and the other innovators, by the end of the eighteenth century, world production of watches grew to more than 350,000 a year. Millions of people now owned watches. Watches were still beyond the means of most laboring people and the millions of poor who fell through the cracks of the new industrial system, but time was no longer the property of the rich. Increasingly it belonged to working people as well, and watch prices were dropping all the time. A cheap Swiss watch that had cost about six francs in 1800 was down to two francs fifteen years later.

Meanwhile, the new nation of the United States was also getting into the watch and clock business. As we have seen, the Industrial Revolution began in England. But Americans were, in 1800, still mainly descended from people of the British Isles, and despite a lot of antagonism between the new nation and the old one, there was also a common culture. Americans spoke English and frequently copied English social ways. In addition, there was an enterprising spirit in America, a sense that all things were possible, produced in part by the abundance that surrounded Americans—

the green fields, vast forests, rivers, lakes, and ocean. Americans felt that anyone who had a good idea and worked hard could succeed.

By the early 1800s the mechanized textile industry was making fortunes for people such as Samuel Slater, an English immigrant who had built the first spinning mill in the United States. Eli Whitney was developing his system of interchangeable parts. And in the first years of the nineteenth century, a clock maker named Eli Terry established a factory for making wooden clocks by machine, as clock parts were bigger than watch parts and did not need to be quite so exact. Others followed Terry's lead, and by the 1830s Chauncy Jerome, with a factory in Bristol, Connecticut, was mass-producing brass clocks that could be sold cheaply to the general public. He began exporting them to England, where they also sold well. It was a harbinger of things to come.

Mass-producing watches, however, proved to be difficult, because the tolerances were much less, as little as 5/1,000 of an inch. The first to succeed was a group led by watchmaker Aaron Dennison. The company he and others started eventually became the famous Waltham Watch Company. Their first efforts at making watch parts by machine failed. Machines of the day were not able to work to the fine tolerances needed for watches. Eventually the company came up with an ingenious plan. Instead of trying to make a pivot the right size to hold a jewel, for example, they decided to cut batches of pivots and jewels as close to standard as they could. They would then sort out both jewels and pivots according to the slight variations in size, and match pivots and jewels accordingly. They used the plan with other parts of the watch as well. Finally they could make watches by machine in large numbers. The Civil War, when millions of soldiers wanted cheap watches, gave the company a large boost.

Inevitably, others followed Waltham's example, among them names still familiar to some, such as Elgin, Waterbury, and Hamilton. By the end of the nineteenth century, the American watch industry was turning out millions of watches annually. Most of them were cheap, some selling for around a dollar.

But they were of surprisingly good quality. Whereas a hundred years earlier machines could not do as fine work as craftsmen working by hand, machine design had improved to the point that machines could do far more accurate work than the best craftspeople's hands. In 1876 a representative of the Swiss watch industry, worried about the growing competition from America, visited the Waltham Company. He took one of their cheapest watches at random and wore it around Paris for six days. The watch had varied by only thirty seconds. He was astonished that so cheap a watch could be so accurate, and he asked one of his leading craftsmen to take it apart for a closer inspection. After examining it for a few days, the craftsman reported, "I am completely overwhelmed; the result is incredible; one would not find one such watch among fifty thousand of our manufacture." After more than six centuries, the handmade timepiece had grown obsolete.

By the late 1800s, then, almost anyone who was not extremely poor could, and did, own a watch. The industrial world was running on time, often to the minute. But it was not the same minute everywhere. People used whatever local time scheme suited them, so that it might be one o'clock in one village, two o'clock in the next, and one-thirty in still another.

So long as people traveled little, and then not very far, they could deal with a variety of time zones. But the new industrial system could not tolerate such a chaotic system. The coming of the railroad, especially, made a standard time scheme necessary. As it was, a train scheduled to arrive at West Centerville at six might not leave East Centerville until seven, due to the differences in the time systems between the two towns.

In 1837 the electric telegraph was invented, and very quickly telegraph lines were run along rail lines. In England, railway companies soon began sending signals to all their stations at once, setting the exact time. Then, in 1847, the British government passed a law requiring all railroads to operate on Greenwich Mean Time. This had the effect of putting the whole nation on Greenwich time. There was, as usual, resistance, but soon the national time system overwhelmed the holdouts. Other nations followed the British example.

The transition was not so easy, though, for nations such as the United

The floor of the Westclox factory in 1906. Westclox was one of the many factories turning out inexpensive clocks and watches for Americans as well as for sale abroad.

States that sprawled across a continent. By 1850 the nation stretched from coast to coast, with sunrise in California coming three hours later than it did on the East Coast. One time system was not going to work for a nation where some people were eating breakfast when others were going out for lunch.

For a while America struggled. Then, in 1883, a conference was held, which divided the country into the four time zones we use today—Eastern, Central, Mountain, and Pacific. Inspired by this example, an international conference was held the next year, which devised the international time system we use today, with Greenwich Mean Time as its base.

By the early twentieth century, with the United States dominating the manufacture of inexpensive watches, the Swiss began specializing in fine watches, especially ones with high-style design and complicated embellishments, such as mechanisms for telling the date or for setting off alarms.

THE WRISTWATCH QUICKLY GAINED IN POPULARITY AS IT WAS SMALL, PORTABLE, AND EASY TO ACCESS. THE INCREASED DEMAND FOR THIS STYLE OF WATCH MEANT EVEN MORE INTENSE COMPETITION AMONG THE VARIOUS COMPANIES VYING FOR THEIR SHARE OF THE SALES. IN AN EFFORT TO DISTINGUISH THEMSELVES AND OUTDO OTHER MANUFACTURERS, SOME COMPANIES' DESIGNS ASSUMED OUTRAGEOUS PROPORTIONS.

Some of these Swiss watches were encrusted with jewels to raise the price and add prestige. Swiss watches emblazoned with gold and diamonds were priced in the millions. Today Switzerland continues to specialize in expensive watches, with Patek, Audemars, Rolex, and Omega being among the most prestigious manufacturers. All the while, Americans continued to turn out excellent mass-produced watches at low prices. Before 1940, Elgin alone was selling almost a million watches per year.

By this time the new wristwatch had replaced the pocket watch. The old pocket watches, especially gold ones, had been prized possessions for millions in the nineteenth and well into the twentieth centuries. Suits of the time were made with watch pockets in the trousers. For safety, pocket watches were attached to cords or chains, also made of matching gold, which were in turn fastened to a short button or other convenient place. These watches often sported fobs, a ribbon or ornament attached to the chain or watch by which the timepiece could be pulled from the pocket. People took great pride in and care of their watches and fobs and left them in their wills to a favorite person. Today these old pocket watches and fobs are collectors' items.

But a wristwatch had a lot of advantages. It was convenient, hard to steal, and left both hands free while a person checked the time. The wristwatch had to be smaller than the pocket watch. A standard pocket watch might be 2 to 3 inches (5 to 7.6 cm) in diameter. By contrast, the largest wristwatches could not be much more than an inch (2.5 cm) in diameter, and fashionable watches for women were much smaller. But by the 1920s the technology to produce good watches of this size had been developed, and the wristwatch drove the pocket watch into the history books. The most famous of the early wristwatches were the Mickey Mouse watches, on which Mickey's arms showed the time. They sold in the millions and are today collectors' items as well. Another innovation, used by many soldiers in World War II, were watches with luminous hands, which could be read in the dark. (This was before it was known that radium was a possible cause of cancer.)

# The International Dateline

The system of time zones may seem simple enough, but it has its complications. Travelers going west around the world at the speed of the Sun, or roughly 1,000 miles (1,609 km) per hour—if this were possible—would move their watches back an hour each time they crossed into a new time zone. When they reached home twenty-four hours later they would discover that it was the same time as it was when they left. However, clearly it would be a day later. To make the days come out accurately, an international dateline was established. It runs through the Pacific Ocean in a somewhat zigzag course, to keep it away from inhabited places as much as possible. A traveler crossing the international dateline discovers it is suddenly the next day, although the time is the same.

Thus, tourists going from New York to Hong Kong on a Tuesday morning—a trip of about twenty hours—will arrive not early on Wednesday, but on Thursday instead.

Wednesday disappears into the date line. However, on the return flight on Tuesday a week later, they would arrive on Tuesday, the same day they left Hong Kong, thus getting in effect, two Tuesdays, and regaining the day they had lost on the trip west.

These wristwatches, like all timepieces before them, had to be wound regularly, in some cases every day. That was not a real problem. People got in the habit of winding their watches frequently, usually far more often than necessary. Inevitably, a self-winding watch was invented. A swinging weight, which would slip back and forth with the ordinary motions of the person wearing the watch, would rewind the spring. Of course, if left lying in a drawer too long, the self-winding watch would run down and have to be reset and shaken a few times to get its gears functioning again.

By the end of World War II, time was, for most people, simply ever present. Not only did most people wear watches, but clocks hung everywhere—in banks, barber shops, schools, railroad stations, the facades of town halls, and on sidewalk stands. In most homes there was a clock in almost every room. The only places where clocks were noticeably absent were in shops and stores where owners hoped their customers would lose track of time, linger, and buy. Whereas eight or nine hundred years ago it was extremely difficult for anybody but astute astronomers to have anything but the haziest idea of what time it was, today it is almost impossible to avoid knowing the time. On vacations some of us have to make a deliberate effort to free ourselves from time by going to cabins in distant woods or cottages on remote coasts. Time has become inescapable.

The early quartz timekeepers, such as this one used at the Greenwich Observatory in 1942, were large and complex. Within a few decades, affordable quartz watches were owned by millions of people.

EIGHT

# Atomic Time for an Atomic World

By 1950, after centuries of effort, the problems of timekeeping had mostly been solved. A consistent calendar was in use virtually everywhere in the world, although religious calendars existed along with it, and some critics hoped to establish a more regular system of months. A huge variety of watches and clocks, most of them accurate to a degree that would have astonished people in John Harrison's day, were available at almost any price. There was, it seemed, nothing further to do with the matter. And yet instead of a dead end, another revolution in timekeeping was about to begin.

To understand this latest change, we need to understand a little bit about electricity. When experimenters were first working with electricity some hundred and fifty years ago, it was learned that a current ran in a circuit from its source—a battery or generator—through a conductor, in most cases a wire, and then back to the source. This direct current worked well enough in small circuits, but it lost its momentum, if we can put it that way, over long distances. The solution was to run the current very quickly back and forth for very short distances. In the United States this current alternates sixty times per second, while in other places the rate is somewhat different. It is called alternating current, usually abbreviated A.C., as opposed to D.C., or direct current.

About a hundred years ago, the famous scientist Pierre Curie discovered that if you ran an alternating current through certain types of crystals they would vibrate rapidly in a regular fashion. Early radios, known as crystal sets, were based on this phenomenon. People soon realized that anything that vibrated in a regular way could be used as a clock. It was also discovered that quartz was a prime material for timekeeping. It was almost unresponsive to changes in temperature and air pressure. A quartz clock was developed in the United States in 1928, and in 1939 one was installed in the Greenwich Observatory that was accurate to within 2/1,000 of a second per day.

These early electronic timekeepers were bulky, expensive to build, and used a lot of power, far more power than could be supplied by a battery small enough to fit in a reasonably sized watch. However, by 1968 the technology had improved enough to make quartz watches feasible. They were expensive, not as reliable as ordinary watches, and not very durable.

But there were those who saw the possibilities, and by 1969 Japanese and American companies were producing electronic watches. Among them was the Seiko Company, still an important name in watchmaking. Soon the size of the watches and the amount of power needed to run them was drastically reduced, and prices started to fall. By 1980 the Japanese in particular were churning out tens of millions of electronic watches annually.

But by this time the technology of timekeeping had gone even further, to the atomic level. In 1948 a so-called atomic clock, based on nitrogen, provided a level of accuracy that would have been unbelievable only twenty years earlier. Then in the 1960s a clock based on the rare element cesium was shown to be accurate to one second every 316,000 years. Experiments are today being conducted with lasers, which are expected to be several times more accurate than cesium clocks.

Is there any point in making clocks of such accuracy, which are in fact more regular than the movements of celestial bodies? Surely nobody needs a clock that tells time within a second per year, much less a second over hundreds of thousands of years. Yet in fact, the ability to measure

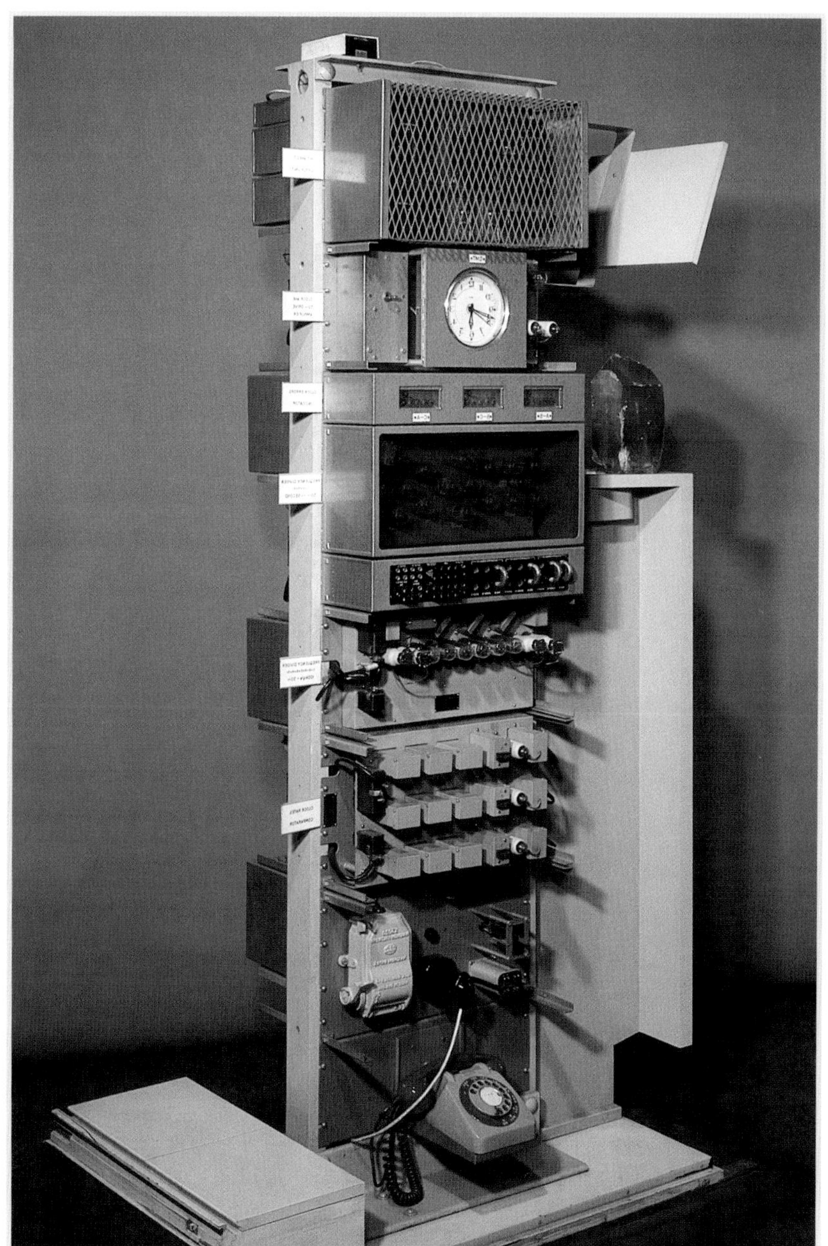

This cesium clock of 1955 was built by English scientists based on research done in the United States. Atomic clocks today can measure time to an almost unbelievable degree of accuracy.

time at this extraordinary level does have a purpose, as a lot of modern devices, such as sonar signals, smart missiles, and global-positioning systems, need to measure time very accurately. Consider this: supersonic airplanes, such as certain modern fighter planes, travel at more than 600 miles (966 km) per hour, which comes out to 1 mile (1.6 km) every 6 seconds, or 880 feet (268 meters) per second. Various types of missiles, such as the smart bombs used in the Persian Gulf War, travel even faster. At these speeds, navigational systems for planes and missiles have to work to a small fraction of a second if they are to come within, let us say, 50 feet (15 m) of a target.

Sonar, which is based on the reflection of sound waves, must measure small differences in sound frequencies. A string in the middle of the piano may vibrate several hundred times per second, and a string higher up, two or three times faster. Electronic keyboards must be able to determine slight differences in frequency vibration in order to play in tune. Scientists studying jazz rhythms have discovered that differences of 1/50 of a second in a beat can affect the "swing" feeling of the music. In sum, much of what we are able to do today in the world of electronics is built on our ability to measure time to an extraordinarily fine degree.

Today we take our ability to measure time for granted. It is simply part of the world we live in. Yet, as should be clear at this point, the scientific revolution of the last few centuries would not have been possible without our increasing ability to measure time. Without clocks, we would almost certainly be living in a world in which most people labored in the fields hoeing, chopping, and plowing, in a world in which cities were small and distances to the stars still a mystery. The clock, as commonplace as it may seem, was one of the crucial inventions of humankind.

# Web Sites

### A Walk through Time
http://physics.nist.gov/GenInt/Time/time.html

### Calendar-Related Links
http://dmoz.org/Kids_and_Teens/School_Time/Reference_Tools/Calendars/

### Clocks and Calendars
http://www.awesomelibrary.org/Classroom/Science/General_Science/Time.html

### Clock-Related Sites
http://www.gomilpitas.com/homeschooling/explore/clocks.htm

### The History of Navigation
http://www.boatsafe.com/kids/navigation.htm

# Bibliography

## Books


FOR STUDENTS

Duncan, David Ewing. *The Calendar: The 5,000-Year Struggle to Align the Clock: Understanding Time and Frequency*. New York: Avon, 1998.

Jespersen, James, and Jane Fitz-Randolph. *From Sundials to Atomic Clocks*. Washington, D.C.: U.S. Department of Commerce, 1999.

Richards, E. G. *Mapping Time: The Calendar and Its History.* New York: Oxford, 1999.

Sobel, Dava. *Longitude*. New York: Penguin, 1995.

Waugh, Alexander. *Time: Its Origin, Its Enigma, Its History*. New York: Carroll & Graf, 2000.

FOR TEACHERS OR ADVANCED READERS

Crosby, Alfred W. *The Measure of Reality: Quantifications of Western Society 1250–1600*. Cambridge, UK: Cambridge University Press, 1997.

Dohrn-van Rossum, Gerhard. *History of the Hour: Clocks and Modern Temporal Orders*. Chicago: University of Chicago Press, 1996.

Landes, David S. *Revolution in Time: Clocks and the Making of the Modern World*. Cambridge, MA: Harvard University Press, 1983.

Lippincott, Kristen. *The Story of Time*. London: Merrell Holberton, 1999.

# Index

Page numbers for illustrations are in **boldface**.

# About the Author

**James Lincoln Collier** has written books for both adults and students on many subjects, among them the prizewinning novel *My Brother Sam Is Dead*. Many of these books, both fiction and nonfiction, have historical themes, including the highly acclaimed Benchmark Books series the Drama of American History, which he wrote with Christopher Collier.

1/ 12/04 3-23-05